The Princeton Review

Word Smart
Executive
Edition

Words for Suits

Books in The Princeton Review Series

Cracking the ACT
Cracking the ACT with Sample Tests on Computer Disk
Cracking the GED
Cracking the GMAT
Cracking the GMAT with Sample Tests on Computer Disk
Cracking the GRE
Cracking the GRE with Sample Tests on Computer Disk
Cracking the GRE Psychology Subject Test
Cracking the LSAT
Cracking the LSAT with Sample Tests on Computer Disk
Cracking the MCAT
Cracking the MCAT with Sample Tests on Computer Disk
Cracking the SAT and PSAT
Cracking the SAT and PSAT with Sample Tests on Computer Disk
Cracking the SAT II: Biology Subject Test
Cracking the SAT II: Chemistry Subject Test
Cracking the SAT II: English Subject Tests
Cracking the SAT II: French Subject Test
Cracking the SAT II: History Subject Tests
Cracking the SAT II: Math Subject Tests
Cracking the SAT II: Physics Subject Test
Cracking the SAT II: Spanish Subject Test
Cracking the TOEFL with Audiocassette

SAT Math Workout
SAT Verbal Workout

Don't Be a Chump!
How to Survive Without Your Parents' Money
Trashproof Resumes

Grammar Smart
Math Smart
Reading Smart
Study Smart
Word Smart: Building an Educated Vocabulary
Word Smart II: How to Build a More Educated Vocabulary
Word Smart Executive Edition: Words for Suits
Word Smart Genius: How to Build an Erudite Vocabulary
Writing Smart

Grammar Smart Junior
Math Smart Junior
Word Smart Junior
Writing Smart Junior

Student Access Guide to America's Top Internships
Student Access Guide to College Admissions
Student Access Guide to the Best Business Schools
Student Access Guide to the Best Law Schools
Student Access Guide to the Best Medical Schools
Student Access Guide to the Best 309 Colleges
Student Access Guide to Paying for College
Student Access Guide to Visiting College Campuses
Student Access Guide: The Big Book of Colleges
Student Access Guide: The Internship Bible

Also available on cassette from Living Language

Grammar Smart
Word Smart
Word Smart II

The Princeton Review

Word Smart
Executive
Edition

Words for Suits

by Liz Buffa

Random House, Inc., New York 1995

ACKNOWLEDGMENTS

The author wishes to thank the many people who had the patience to sit with her during this time and explain their own business terms—a special thanks to Dominick Buffa, David Bradley, and Vincent Tortorici in this regard.

Thanks again to Chris Kensler, Lee Elliott, Carrie Smith, Alex Costley, Chris Scott, Illeny Maaza, and Meher Khambata for their grace under pressure and excellent work putting this all together.

CONTENTS

INTRODUCTION

WHY BE "WORD SMART"?

Imagine this scenario: you're in a meeting. Executives in pin-striped suits are arguing wildly about the wisdom of selling their leasehold on a property to the nefarious Acme Corp. They all turn, simultaneously it seems, and ask, "Hey, what's your opinion?" Well, you'd probably feel better about the whole thing if you knew what they were talking about.

Or what if that computer department head comes shuffling into your cubicle mumbling something about Archie, Veronica, and Gopher, and you mistakenly repeat it around the office water cooler as the hottest new gossip around? Ah, if only you knew that Archie and Veronica are computer programs!

Everyone, no matter how skilled or savvy, has a time in business when she is stymied by some term. No matter what type of business you're in, there's some area that has always confused you. The problem is, when you are in a meeting or trying to answer a question or convince someone that you are the person for the job, you don't like to say things like "Huh? What's a leasehold, anyway?" What you need is a quick reference that will give you a basic definition without assuming you have a Ph.D. in Business Management.

WHY YOU NEED THIS BOOK

There are plenty of business books on the shelves of your library. Have you looked at any of them? They take pages and pages to explain even the simplest term. Or they assume you have a lot of knowledge you may not have. When you're on the phone with a client or sitting in a seminar, you need a quick answer.

How This Book Is Organized

We've arranged business terms into six different categories. This way, you can skim through and see like terms in the same chapter. The seven categories are:

BUSINESS AND MANAGEMENT

The basics of business—production, management, sales, and shipping. Here you'll find terms dealing with production methods, employee and employer issues, management technique and theory, and sales and shipping.

COMPUTERS

From personal computers to the Internet—the terms you'll need to know to buy computers, use them, and learn about services.

MONEY AND FINANCE

Banking, stocks, bonds, mutual funds, futures, and options. A quick guide to the myriad confusing terms that deal with money and spending it.

REAL ESTATE

This chapter sorts through the most common, confusing terms, whether you are trying to learn about buying, selling, renting, or financing real estate.

TAXES

Ah, the inevitable: all the different taxes, from income to Social Security. Included in this section are terms about tax-free things such as retirement and pension funds as well.

INSURANCE

Health, Life, and Casualty—the basic terms you need to know to understand what kind of policy you are buying.

ACRONYMS AND ABBREVIATIONS

Why is it that business people more than any other group like to use acronyms? The appearance of efficiency? The joy of using a lingo that only the insiders will get? Whatever the reason, this list will decipher the strangest and most common abbreviations you are likely to hear.

TALK THE TALK

Once you've familiarized yourself with the terms in this book, you'll have a six-figure vocabulary that will enable you to talk the talk. If you can walk the walk, you'll be a word-smart executive in no time.

Chapter 1

BUSINESS AND MANAGEMENT

Do you know,
Considering the market, there are more
Poems produced than any other thing?
No wonder poets sometimes have to *seem*
So much more businesslike than businessmen.
Their wares are so much harder to get rid of.

—Robert Frost,
"New Hampshire"

ABC METHOD

A way of managing inventory that gives more weight to more-expensive merchandise. "A" is the most expensive inventory, "B" is less expensive, and "C" is the least expensive.

The XYZ Corp. always used the *ABC method* when they catalogued their inventory so that they would know which items needed the most time and care.

ABILITY TO PAY

In general business terms, this refers to a company's ability to handle financial demands from their operating income. As a policy, some businesses (usually public or not-for-profit) charge on a sliding scale according to "ability to pay," meaning that the less the income of an individual or company, the less the charge for service.

After the rumors of financial mismanagement, the local chapter of the Slime workers' union was concerned about Acme Corps. *ability to pay.*

The Smiths liked to use the local public health clinic whose services were offered on an *"ability to pay"* scale.

ABSORB

If a business does not pass a cost along to the consumer, it is said to absorb that cost.

Tweezerman had to *absorb* the expense of the electric company's rate increase; they didn't want to raise the price of their tweezers.

ACCORD AND SATISFACTION

If you pay money or offer something in return for another company to absolve your debt to them, you are asking for *accord and satisfaction*.

Since Acme Corp. would never pay off their debt, L-Mart accepted two-thousand "slime balls" as *accord and satisfaction* and wiped the debt from their records.

ACCOUNTABILITY

A management system of responsibility. An associate vice president may be accountable to a senior vice president, who is accountable to an executive vice president. Each person in the chain must account for his or her actions and results to the next person in the chain.

Jane was *accountable* to her senior loan officer for her weekly budget and operations report.

ACCOUNTS PAYABLE

The list of a company's outstanding debts. Typically, regular payments such as salary, rent, and debt service would not be included in accounts payable.

The assistant bookkeeper, Kate, printed out a list of *accounts payable* for her boss; it included bills for supplies, service contracts, and merchandise.

ACCOUNTS RECEIVABLE

The money that is owed to you.

Even though Zippy Corp. didn't have much money in its accounts, it was able to get a line of credit because the amount of its *accounts receivable* was so high.

ACCRETION

Any growth in a company's assets. Accretion may occur due to expansion or an increase in the value of a company's investment.

When the diamond shortage hit, Diamonds "R" Us experienced a huge *accretion* because all the diamonds in its stock tripled in value.

ACROSS THE BOARD

An event or action that affects all aspects of a company or group is said to happen across the board.

Across the board cuts affected all the employees at Acme Corp.

Across the board increases raised all the prices of Zippy Corp.'s new line of products.

AFFIDAVIT

A legal document, made under oath, that attests to something.

The lawyers told the employee to file an *affidavit* with the court attesting to her complaints of unfair hiring practices at Acme Corp.

AFFIRMATIVE ACTION

A program that requires a certain percentage of minority hiring, usually reflecting some past discriminatory actions on the part of an employer.

When the local court ruled that the city hiring programs had been discriminatory, it instituted a plan of *affirmative action* that required that future hiring reflect the percentage of minority population in the city.

AGGLOMERATION

The act of putting together different companies into one large conglomeration.

The agglomeration of Acme Corp., XYZ Corp., and Zippy Corp. formed the giant conglomerate of SXZ, Inc.

AGGREGATE
AGGREGATE INCOME
AGGREGATE SUPPLY
AGGREGATE DEMAND

The aggregate refers to the sum of the parts. Aggregate income is the total income a company acquires. Aggregate supply is an economic term for the total goods and services supplied to a market at a given time. Aggregate demand is the total demand for goods and services in a market.

GNP is one example of an *aggregate income.*

Economists like to compare the *aggregate demand* with the *aggregate supply* in a country to gauge its economic status.

AIR BILL OR AIRWAY BILL

The airfreight version of a bill of lading.

Fed Air Shipping always had *airway bills* attached to each carton to ensure that the contents were correct.

AIRFREIGHT

Using airplanes to transport freight. Airfreight is more convenient but much more expensive than truck or rail freight.

Federal Express is one of the largest *airfreight* shippers in the country.

ALLOCATION OF RESOURCES

This is one of the key factors in economic study: how a limited amount of resources (both physical resources and employees) are dispersed among the people and companies who need them to make products and services, and then from the producer to the consumers of the products and services.

The *allocation of resources* after the earthquake was so difficult that prices rose sky-high.

ALLOWANCE

A price reduction given to a retailer in compensation for something. A brokerage allowance assumes, for example, that a certain number of items may be broken in shipping. Retail display allowance is a price break in exchange for a better selling spot on the shelves.

L-Mart liked to order from Zippy Corp., who was willing to give a generous retail display *allowance*: Zippy cut the price if L-Mart displayed the merchandise at the front register.

AMERICAN FEDERATION OF LABOR—CONGRESS OF INDUSTRIAL ORGANIZATIONS (AFL-CIO)

The largest labor union in the United States.

The *AFL-CIO* represents many tradespeople; the presidential candidate hoped to get their support by having a pro-labor platform.

ANNUAL DEBT SERVICE

(see **debt service**)

ANNUALIZED RATE

To take any rate given in a certain time frame and convert it to a rate for the year.

When Rip-Off Retailers offered a "low, low" interest rate of only 2 percent, Marty was quick to point out that it was a monthly rate and that the *annualized rate* would be 24 percent—no bargain.

ANTITRUST
ANTITRUST LAWS

Laws designed to promote fair trade practices by outlawing things like price fixing, monopolies, price discrimination, and similar unfair business practices.

A small segment of zipper producers was brought up on charges of price fixing, illegal under our *antitrust laws*.

ARBITER
ARBITRATOR

Impartial third parties used to settle disputes. They have become very popular in labor disputes in recent years. Arbiters must bring their decision to the court that appointed them for a final okay; arbitrators have authority to make a final decision.

The *arbitrator* for the contract negotiations between the employees and Acme Corp. sat up all night with both sides trying to compromise on the issue of overtime.

ARREARS

If something is overdue, it is said to be in arrears.

The account executive finally turned over all the accounts in *arrears* to a collection agency.

ASSEMBLY LINE

A method of production that gives each worker one specific task that he or she repeats; each worker represents one step in the production process.

When Zippy Corp. changed to an *assembly line* manufacturing process, each worker, who previously had made one complete zipper, had to be retrained to perform just one step in the production of zippers.

BACKLOG

The monetary value of any orders a business holds but has yet to fill. Looking at the backlog is a good way for a company to assess how efficient or timely they are, and how much income they can expect in the short term.

"Our business is doing well!" insisted the CEO of Acme Corp. at the board meeting. "Just take a look at our *backlog*—we have orders of almost a million dollars waiting to be filled."

BAIT AND SWITCH

An unethical (and sometimes illegal) practice of enticing unwary consumers with the promise of a certain product or price and then either talking them out of that product or being out of stock, with the intent of selling them a more expensive one.

Z-Mart was accused of using an illegal *bait-and-switch* pricing policy when they admitted that they were always out of stock on their $159 big-screen televisions yet tried to sell their customers the $2,000 model.

BALANCE OF TRADE

The difference between exports and imports for a given country at a given time. If the country exports more than it imports, it has a favorable balance of trade. If it imports more, the balance is unfavorable.

When the small country of Zeanna suddenly found a booming worldwide market for their hand-carved beads, they benefited from a favorable *balance of trade*.

BALANCE SHEET

A financial statement listing all a company's or an individual's assets balanced against its liabilities and equity.

A quick glance at their *balance sheet* told the executives at XYZ that they had a lot of equity in their business.

BANKRUPTCY

When an individual or company does not have enough money to pay its debts. Chapter 11 bankruptcy is voluntary bankruptcy; chapter 7 is involuntary. In either case, a court helps the company or individual to settle debts.

After Acme Corp. declared *bankruptcy*, it was able to settle its bills by paying ten cents on every dollar it owed.

BAR CODE

Those funky lines and numbers you see on just about every product in the world. A computer scans a *bar code* for data such as price and inventory information.

BASE-YEAR ANALYSIS

A method of analyzing economic trends that uses one year as the yardstick against which all others are measured. Using the "constant dollars" from one year lets analysts see how much things have gone up or down, without inflation.

The Gross National Product uses the prices of products from a certain *base-year* analysis so that economists are able to see if the country is really producing more or less, rather than if prices have just gone up or down.

BEAR HUG

A takeover offer that is well above the current market value of stock.

When the board of trustees at Irate Corp. tried to resist the *bear hug* takeover attempt made by Acme Corp., shareholders reminded the board that they had to accept an offer that was in the best interests of the investors.

BELLWETHER

Any particular investment that is considered to be an indicator of the stock market's overall condition.

Since Giant Machines Corp. was owned and invested in by the most important investors in the stock market, its share price was considered a *bellwether* for the market's condition.

BILL OF LADING (BOL)

The contract that shows the contents, by amount and weight, of what you are shipping. The bill of lading is not a bill at all, but rather a table of contents for the shipment.

Before accepting the shipment, Tizzy Corp. employees were supposed to check the contents of all packages against the bill of lading to be sure that everything was in the shipment.

BIG-TICKET ITEMS

Expensive retail items that are almost always purchased on credit.

Retail sales at Cheapo Stores Inc. were up in the third quarter due to the interest-free financing they offered on such *big-ticket items* as washer-dryers, entertainment systems, and refrigerators.

BLACK MARKET

Items that are sold illegally are said to be sold on the black market. Usually, black market items are expensive because they are restricted by the government or some shortage of supply.

Jan had to pay top dollar for the cigarettes she bought on the *black market* during the government's rationing.

BLUE-COLLAR WORKER

Tradespeople. Typically, blue-collar workers have the types of jobs that might require a uniform, such as a delivery person, a construction worker, or a plumber.

The hourly wages for *blue-collar workers* in our company increased when the union negotiated their contract.

BOILERPLATE

A form in which the specifics are entered to customize it. Boilerplate may even refer to any language which would be standard in any contract or document.

When you go over those leases, don't bother reading the introductory clauses; they're all just legal *boilerplate*.

BOOK VALUE

A company's worth if all its assets were sold and its debts were paid off.

The *book value* on Zippy Corp. would certainly be great if it were to liquidate—it's got such valuable property with practically no debt at all.

BOONDOGGLE

An unnecessary business project. Boondoggles are sometimes created to give someone a job or do someone a favor.

"That whole Shmendrick Project is just a *boondoggle* to keep the boss's nephew employed," Smithers told her new secretary.

BOTTOM LINE

The final profit or loss on a project; a plan's cost to a company.

After listening to a sales pitch on the necessity of water coolers in each office, the president of Zippy asked the salesperson, "What's the *bottom line* here? What will this cost me?"

BRAND (NAME)
BRAND ASSOCIATION
BRAND LOYALTY

A name, symbol, or phrase that identifies a product as coming from a certain company. If a product has a high brand association, that means that one company is associated with that brand more than any other.

Band-aids, Kleenex, Singer, and Xerox are all brands that have such high brand association that their names are synonymous with the products they represent.

Brand loyalty occurs when people are loyal to a brand name and associate it with quality and value.

Because her family always bought Toyotas, Alice had a great deal of brand loyalty to those cars—she had grown up riding in them.

BROKERAGE ALLOWANCE

(see **allowance**)

BUYBACK AGREEMENT

Any clause in a contract which guarantees that the seller will buy the item back from the purchaser in a certain time frame.

L-Mart insisted on a *buyback agreement*, so that Acme Corp. would buy back any unsold slimeballs within six months.

BUY-OUT

Purchasing the controlling share of a company's stock.

XYZ Corp. tried to *buy out* ABC Corp. by purchasing up large blocks of ABC stock.

CAPACITY

How much a company can produce.

What's Zippy Corp.'s Capacity?

Zippy's capacity may be measured in one of five ways:

1. *Ideal capacity.* If everything were perfect—with no waste or breakdown—how much Zippy Corp. would produce.
2. *Normal capacity.* The average of Zippy's actual production over several years.
3. *Planned capacity.* What Zippy can expect to make in one specific normal year.
4. *Operating capacity.* What Zippy makes in a normal time period (part of a year: monthly, weekly, daily operating capacity).
5. *Practical Capacity.* How well Zippy could do, taking into account some normal inefficiency and losses.

CAPITAL
CAPITAL EXPENDITURES
CAPITAL IMPROVEMENTS

Capital is the general term for all the factors needed for production. In finance, *capital* refers to the money needed for a project. Capital expenditures are purchases of new equipment that will last more than a year; if you improve a piece of machinery or equipment to increase its efficiency, you are instituting capital improvements.

After modernizing the plant with a number of *capital expenditures* and *capital improvements*, ABC Corp. went to the bank to ask for more *capital*.

CAPITALISM

An economic system based on the principles of free competition, private ownership, and profit maximization.

The transition from a communist economy to a *capitalist* one was difficult: the citizens were not used to profit-making and competition.

CAPITALIZE

When you capitalize an asset, you take an income stream that you expect to receive from that asset, and divide it by an interest (or capitalization) rate to arrive at a present value for the item. *Capitalize* may also refer to taking advantage of a situation.

When Zippy Corp. *capitalized* the income they could expect to receive from the new factory, they decided that it would be worth only about $100,000.

Acme Corp. *capitalized* on the new slime craze after the success of the childrens' movie *The Slime King*.

CARTEL

A cartel is formed when independent companies group together to agree on trade restrictions.

OPEC, the oil *cartel*, agreed to restrict the amount of oil that would be released on the market.

CASE STUDIES

A method used in many business schools to analyze business decisions. Some case studies present hypothetical situations a business may be in; some present actual occurrences in certain companies. Students look at the information, analyze the data, and typically make theoretical decisions.

The most important class Jane took her first year in B school was Case Studies—it gave her a sense of what type of decisions needed to be made.

CASH COW

A business that generates lots and lots of money.

That division of Zippy Corp. is a real *cash cow*—they can't pay out dividends fast enough!

CASH-FLOW ANALYSIS

A cash-flow analysis looks at how the cash reserves in a company are affected during a specified period, such as where the cash came from (sources) and how it was spent.

The accountants at ABC Corp. gave the CEO a *cash-flow analysis* so she could see how the money had been spent in that quarter.

CASH ON DELIVERY OR COLLECT ON DELIVERY (COD)

If you order a shipment or delivery COD, you must be ready with either cash or a certified check to pay for it at the time of delivery.

Mike was so embarrassed when the delivery person said the package was ordered *COD* and he didn't have the money to pay for it.

CAVEAT EMPTOR

Latin for "Let the buyer beware." In other words, you often buy things at your own risk—you need to beware of what the seller may tell you.

Although *caveat emptor* is a smart way to do business, a seller is usually bound by law to inform the purchaser of any problems with a product.

CHAPTER 7 (OF THE 1978 BANKRUPTCY ACT)

If a business files under Chapter 7, a court appointed trustee will take over the business, liquidate assets, and do what is possible to minimize loss to the investors.

N-Mart had no choice but to file *Chapter 7* bankruptcy and close its doors.

CHAPTER 11 (OF THE 1978 BANKRUPTCY ACT)

Chapter 11, on the other hand, leaves the business in the hands of the owners and helps to reorganize and keep the business going.

Due to a major setback, M-Mart filed under *Chapter 11* bankruptcy and reorganized so that it might pull through this financial trouble.

CHIEF EXECUTIVE OFFICER (CEO)

The head honcho in a company. The CEO reports only to the board of directors.

When Rita was appointed *CEO* of Zippy Corp. by the board of directors, she knew that she'd finally realized the pinnacle of success.

CHIEF FINANCIAL OFFICER (CFO)

An officer of a company who can make financial decisions and authorize expenses.

The *CFO* at Zippy Corp. signed each check that went out.

CHIEF OPERATING OFFICER (COO)

The person who runs the day-to-day stuff around a company. The COO may also hold the title of president.

The *COO* at Zippy Corp. oversees all the acquisitions and hiring done in the company.

CLONE

Any product that is identical to another product.

In the 1980s, IBM computer *clones* littered the market. They were popular because they were often less expensive than IBM computers, but could use all the software designed for IBM.

CLOSELY HELD CORPORATION

A company in which the stock is divided among a few shareholders.

One of the reasons that XYZ Corp. was able to make so many decisions so quickly was that they were a *closely held corporation*.

COLD CANVASS
COLD CALL

A sales technique of going door to door or calling a list of people who have not requested your services.

One of the most difficult things for the sales force at ABC Corp. was the *cold canvass*, where they went from store to store to sell their merchandise; only one store in ten was even interested in listening to the pitch.

COMMODITY

Any physical thing that is bought or sold; gems, grains, food and such are all commodities. They are often traded on the commodities market.

Because of the flood, there was such a shortage in many of the basic *commodities*—food and clothing—that the cost of living in Za-Za-land sky-rocketed.

COMMUNISM

An economic system based on the ideal of ownership of production tools by the workers. In practice, communism is more likely to be a situation in which business is state owned and prices and supply are controlled.

The fall of *communism* in many countries has led to the idea that state-owned business does not work as efficiently as it could.

COMPETITION

Rivalry. In a healthy market, there is free competition between companies in each industry. The people you compete with are called your *competitors*.

If there is enough *competition* in a market, consumers will purchase the best quality product at the best price; that's how *competition* helps to make production more efficient.

CONCILIATION

A process used in labor disputes. The aim of conciliation is to get management and labor to sit and talk with the hope that they can work out their problems.

The arbitrator was hoping to get some *conciliation* between the striking workers and management, who were not even talking at that time.

CONSIGNEE

In shipping, the receiver of the goods.

L-Mart, the *consignee,* accepted its order of 2,000 slime balls from Acme Corp.

CONSIGNOR

The shipper of the goods.

Acme Corp, the *consignor,* shipped 2,000 slime balls to L-Mart.

CONSTANT DOLLARS

The value of the dollar in a base year. If 1990 is chosen as the base for constant dollars, any inflation or decrease in the value of the dollar after that year is adjusted so all actual purchasing power can be compared from year to year.

The economists at the government offices released figures for this year's Gross National Product, as measured in *constant dollars,* so that they could compare it to last year's GNP.

CONSUMER

The user of goods and services. Sometimes the consumer of a good is the purchaser; sometimes the purchaser buys the product for someone else to use.

Ms. Finnegan bought toys for the youngest *consumers* in her household: her two- and three-year-old children.

CONSUMER CONFIDENCE

A measure of how typical consumers feel about their current situation and their faith in the future. If people feel good about where they are and where they're going, consumer confidence is said to be high and the economy will benefit. Even if there is economic recovery, if people are lacking confidence, they will be hesitant to spend.

Consumer confidence surveys generally check a number of things: how people feel about their job security, whether they would buy big-ticket items, or whether they are willing to spend on short-term purchases.

CONSUMER PRICE INDEX (CPI)

A monthly index from the Bureau of Labor Statistics on what it costs for food, shelter, and other essentials; it is used to adjust Social Security payments and cost-of-living increases.

Food, clothing, medical care, shelter, entertainment and even baby-sitting costs are all in the "basket of goods" the Bureau of Labor Statistics uses to calculate the *CPI.*

CONSUMER RESEARCH

Analysis done using such tools as focus groups (small groups of representative consumers), interviews, and surveys to get information about how people use products, why they buy them, how they respond to marketing campaigns, etc.

Zippy Corp. employed the prestigious marketing firm Consumers "R" Us to do some *consumer research* regarding the reaction to their new line of zippers.

CONSUMPTION FUNCTION

Ratio of how much people consume to how much they earn.

Economists calculate the *consumption function* as a gauge of consumer confidence.

COST/BENEFIT ANALYSIS (OR STUDY)

A study that weighs the cost of a certain investment or business action against all the costs involved, including costs that may not be monetary, such as inconvenience.

Market Corp.'s *cost/benefit analysis,* which weighed our loss of efficiency for three months, made us realize that the expansion was not a good idea.

COST METHOD
COST-OF-LIVING INDEX

(see **consumer price index**)

CROSS-MERCHANDISING

A method of display that places similar items in the same area. The idea is that the buyers may cross to a related product made by the same company.

Stickey's Peanut Butter found through market research that *cross-merchandising* their other products, such as Stickey's Marshmallow Stuff and Stickey's Gooey Jelly, got a high percentage of consumer crossover.

DEBT COVERAGE RATIO

Net operating income divided by annual debt service.

The bank always calculated the *debt coverage ratio* to see if an income-producing property had enough income to justify a certain loan amount.

DEBT SERVICE

Interest on loans along with any payments on the principal due within a year's time.

One look at Acme Corp.'s annual *debt service* led the bank to believe that the company had already overextended itself with credit.

DE FACTO

Latin for "in fact." Used to refer to things that exist "in fact" but not through any legal authority.

Zippy Corp. was a *de facto* corporation; the owners had never filed the legal papers to incorporate the company.

DECELERATE

To slow down.

By most predictions, the economy will *decelerate* in 1995; all the leading economic indicators are on the downswing.

DEFLATION

A decline in prices; the opposite of inflation.

It's been a long time since we've had a period of *deflation* across the board in this economy even though prices have fallen in certain sectors, such as technology.

DEREGULATION

A process of removing any government regulation on a certain industry. The idea of deregulation is to let the market determine prices and supply.

Some feel that the *deregulation* of the banking industry led to the downfall of many of the Savings and Loans in the 1980s.

DIMINISHING RETURNS

The law stating that after a certain point, adding more people or machinery to the production process will not yield an equal amount of greater returns.

"If we've doubled our production with a work force that's twice as big as before, we should quadruple our production if we hire four times as many people," suggested Smithers.

"Haven't you ever heard of the law of *diminishing returns*? We'll have more overcrowding and waste, so we won't get all that much more work done," replied Brown.

DIRECT MARKETING

Selling to a customer individually. Things like package inserts, door-to-door sales, phone sales, and newspaper and magazine inserts are all examples of direct marketing. The promotion targets a certain segment of the population, whether people on a mailing list or subscribers to a certain magazine.

The ad department at XYZ Corp. suggested a *direct marketing* campaign of sending catalogues to all the people on the *Sewing Digest* mailing list.

DISCLOSURE

A release of company information.

Acme Corp. had to make a full *disclosure* to the SEC before they issued stock, so potential investors would know the soundness of the organization.

DISCOUNT

A reduction in price. The amount of the discount is the difference between the full price and what is paid.

Zippy offered a 10 percent *discount* on all invoices that were paid within thirty days.

DOWNSCALE

Selling a less expensive, less prestigious type of merchandise.

The retailers in the new Snob Hill Mall were dismayed at the *downscale* merchandising of the new Clothes!Clothes!Clothes! store.

DOWNSIZING

The process of making a company smaller; letting go of employees.

The new employees at Acme Corp. were understandably worried about their jobs when the rumor went out that, due to a bad year, Acme would be *downsizing* its workforce by 20 percent.

From The "And You Thought You'd Know When You'd Been Fired" School

Wesley Poriotis, CEO of New York executive recruiter Wesley, Brown and Bartle, has accumulated twenty-eight euphemisms for firing an employee. So, if your boss tell you they need to de-layer and you can assist your company in rightsizing itself, run for the door.
—*Business Week*, March 7, 1994

DRY GOODS

Clothing, fabrics, textiles, and bedding.

The shipment of *dry goods* arrived, packed with twenty yards each of cotton, silk, and rayon.

EARNINGS

Income gotten the old fashioned way—you earn it. Earned income is contrasted to income you get from investments (such as interest income).

Marge's *earnings* this year were up—thank goodness, because her interest from investments had dropped to practically nothing.

ECONOMIC BASE

The industries that employ people in a particular area.

The *economic base* in Smallville was severely injured when Giant Corp. Industries closed its local plant.

ECONOMIC LIFE

The life expectancy of a piece of machinery.

Mr. Smoothie, the sales person, assured us that the new punch-hole machine on the assembly line has an *economic life* of almost fifty years.

ELASTICITY OF SUPPLY
ELASTICITY OF DEMAND

How responsive something is to a price change. The supply of widgets is elastic if a change in widget price causes the supply to increase or decrease. The demand for widgets is elastic if a change in widget price affects how much people want to buy the widget.

The producers of widgets were not concerned about the recent price increases; they believed that demand for their product was *elastic*, and they would sell just as many as before.

EMBARGO

When the government prohibits trade with or shipments to a certain country. Embargoes may be for security reasons, political reasons, or economic reasons.

The president recently enacted an *embargo* against Za-Za-land, after the political coup d'etat there.

ENTERPRISE

Business; it may also refer specifically to new business.

There was a surge in *enterprise* in Smallville as new entrepreneurs came in to fill the vacant office space left when Giant Corp. Industries moved out.

ENTERPRISE ZONE

An area designated by a municipality to give benefits to business. They may offer tax credit, low financing, etc., to encourage business in depressed areas.

Although Urban Inc. wanted to move out, the formation of an *enterprise zone* made it worth their while to stay in the depressed city of Midville.

ENTREPRENEUR

Someone who starts a business; the term is often associated with a risk taker.

It was the *entrepreneurial* spirit of the early businessmen in this country that brought about much of the eventual prosperity.

EQUAL CREDIT OPPORTUNITY ACT
EQUAL EMPLOYMENT OPPORTUNITY COMMISSION (EEOC)
EQUAL OPPORTUNITY EMPLOYER

All of these terms refer to federal legislation that prohibits discrimination based on sex, age, race, religion, or ethnic background. An Equal Opportunity Employer is one who has pledged to follow the rules of non-discrimination.

Jack was thrilled to see that the businesses in Smallville were all *Equal Opportunity Employers*.

EQUITY

The value of your investment minus any debt held against it.

When Zan and Marta deducted the $50,000 mortgage they had against their property, worth almost $200,000, they had $150,000 in *equity*.

EXPENSE

A cost associated with doing business. An expense account is an allowance given to executives and salespeoples for travel and business entertainment.

When *expenses* rose so dramatically during the metal shortage, Zippy Corp. had to raise its prices.

Salespersons at Zippy had to take a cut in their *expense accounts* as well; no more business-class airline tickets.

EXPORTS

Materials shipped out of a country.

Japan's steel *exports* increased 1.8 percent in October of this year.

FAST TRACK

The expression for a way of promoting specific people up through the company ranks, moving them past others who may have been above them.

"That Jones certainly is on the *fast track*," commented Smithers. "He's already in charge of the department he started in."

FEASIBILITY STUDY

A study, usually done by an independent company, determining how well a proposed project might be able to fulfill objectives. Feasibility studies vary from project to project, but they may include things like probable demand for the project, current supplies, legal considerations, probable profits, etc.

Before investing in any new venture, Money Co. insisted that a full *feasibility study* be done.

FIDUCIARY

Any person entrusted to hold or invest money or other assets for a third party; for example, an executor of a will. Depending on state law, fiduciaries may be limited as to what they can do with the assets they are entrusted to hold. The word may be used to describe the person, or as an adjective to describe the responsibility.

The court appointed a *fiduciary* to help the company dispose of its assets.

The executor's *fiduciary* responsibility included liquidating the investments so that they might be dispersed.

FINANCIAL STATEMENT

A report of a company's balance sheet, income statement, and net worth.

Zippy Corp. published its annual *financial statement* for investors.

FINDER'S FEE

A finder brings together parties for a business deal. Typically, the finder will help with the negotiations and consummation of the deal. You pay the finder's fee to that person if and when the deal is done.

Jane was thrilled to pay a *finder's fee* to Mr. Brown when he found her some limited partners who were willing to bring in the needed capital for her expansion.

FIRST IN, FIRST OUT (FIFO)

A way of valuing your inventory and calculating your taxable profit. When inventory is sold, the cost of the what you bought first is charged against what was sold before later purchases are charged. It's easier to see with numbers, so check out the chart below.

Dolls! Dolls! Dolls!

Inventory and profit valuation figured using the *FIFO* method:

January: purchased 10 dolls at a cost of $2 each
June: purchased 10 dolls at a cost of $6 each
For the years: old 16 dolls at a price of $20 each
Gross sales: $320.00

In the *FIFO* method, we charge the first ones sold against the first ones purchased; of those 16 dolls, 10 were from the $2 batch and 6 were from the $6 batch. In total, the dolls cost:

$10 \times 2 = \$20.00$
$\underline{6 \times 6 = \$36.00}$
$\quad\quad\quad\quad \$56.00$

Total Profit: $320—$56 = $264.00

Now, look at inventory and profit valuation using the *LIFO* method

January: purchased 10 dolls at a cost of $2 each
June: purchased 10 dolls at a cost of $6 each
For the year sold: 16 dolls at a price of $20 each
Gross sales: $320.00

The last items bought are charged against inventory first. Of the 16 dolls sold, assume that the first 10 were the $6.00 dolls, and the last 6 were the $2.00. So:

$10 \times 6 = \$60.00$
$\underline{6 \times 2 = \$12.00}$
$\quad\quad\quad\quad \$72.00$

Total Profit: $320–$72 = $248.00

Note: In a period of inflation, the FIFO method increases taxable profits. LIFO is more popular when prices are rising, because it reduces the amount of income tax a company pays.

FISCAL YEAR

Any twelve-month period that may or may not coincide with a calendar year.

The local school board ran its *fiscal year* beginning in September and ending in August, so that it would coincide with the school year.

FIXED COST

Any cost that doesn't vary with changes in business volume. Most salaries, rents, etc., are fixed costs.

Unfortunately for Zippy Corp., most of its major expenses were *fixed costs*, so they could not withstand a long period of poor sales.

FLAGSHIP

A store, office, or product that is either the most important, largest, best-selling, or most identified with its company.

When Zippy Corp. redesigned the Zippy Zipper, its *flagship* product, most consumers were quite distraught.

The company headquarters is located at our *flagship* offices in Memphis, Tennessee.

FRANCHISE

A license granted to an owner-operator of a business to use a company's name and product. The license typically binds the operator to buy only the company's products, merchandising, sales, and promotions. The owner-operator is the *franchisee*, the parent company is the *franchiser*.

When George decided to buy a fast-food *franchise*, he investigated all the major ones that weren't in his town: McDonald's, Dunkin' Donuts, Carvel, Roy Rogers, and KFC.

FREE ALONGSIDE SHIP (FAS)

The seller is responsible for a shipment from his factory to the dock. The buyer assumes responsibility from there.

When Acme Corp. sent its new shipment to J-Mart, they paid for shipments *FAS*.

FREE ON BOARD (FOB)

Delivery charges: if you pay for something FOB, it is for the price of the merchandise as it sits at the dock. If you want it delivered somewhere, that will be extra.

Since it was his first day on the job, Edgar didn't know that *FOB* New Orleans meant that the delivery of yo-yos was only paid for to the dock in New Orleans. Now he had to find the extra money to have them sent to the store.

FREIGHT COLLECT

Charges paid by the receiver of the goods.

When L-Mart received the order *freight collect*, they were annoyed to think that Acme Corp. sent the goods but left the freight charges to be paid by L-Mart.

FREIGHT DELIVERY

Shipping charges: if you want a shipment to include delivery charges from the dock to your door, you want "freight delivery."

To save having to calculate delivery charges, Zippy Corp. always ordered its merchandise *freight delivery*.

FRINGE BENEFIT

(see **perquisite**)

GARNISH

To take money out of someone's salary in order to pay a court settlement. The person who takes the money out (usually the employer) is the *garnishee*; the court order to have the money taken out is called a *garnishment*.

When XYZ Corp. won the suit against Ms. Yellow, they had her wages *garnished* to pay the settlement.

GENERAL PARTNER

Any partner who is not a limited partner. A general partner has liability in a business and has a say in how the business is run.

Rose wanted a *general partner* when she began her new business, someone who would help with money but also help run the company.

GENERIC BRAND

A plain, unadvertised product.

Bill always bought *generic* products in the supermarket; they were not advertised and therefore were much less expensive than regular, well-known brands.

GOLDEN HANDSHAKE
GOLDEN PARACHUTE

Both deal with plans for leaving a company: A *golden handshake* is an incentive package for early retirement. A *golden parachute* is a special deal ensuring that when an executive retires or if her job is lost, she will receive a nice package of benefits, such as stock options, severance pay, etc.

When GHI Corp. had to downsize, they offered all the highly paid executives *golden handshakes* if they chose early retirement.

Before signing with Zippy Corp., Smithers insisted on a *golden parachute* clause in his contract, in case the company was bought out.

GROSS

The total before deducting things like taxes, expenses, etc.

Jan's *gross* annual income was $50,000—quite a bit more than her after-tax income of about $30,000.

GROSS NATIONAL PRODUCT (GNP)

The total value of a country's annual output of goods and services.

The *GNP* for this year was much lower than last year—no doubt a result of the recession.

GROSS REVENUE
GROSS SALES

The total sales amount, without any adjustments for discounts or returns.

JayMart gave figures for its *gross sales* for the fiscal year; the figures appeared high because none of the numerous discounts were figured in.

GUARANTEE

A promise by a manufacturer or retailer to fix or replace a product within a certain time frame. Some retailers offer price guarantees—a promise to refund the difference if the consumer sees a product elsewhere at a lower price.

"You won't find better prices or service anywhere! We *guarantee* it for one year from the date of your purchase!" claimed the ads at L-Mart.

HARD GOODS

Durable goods, such as cars, furniture, appliances, etc.

The price of *hard goods* had increased over the past year, due to the recession in the large retail market.

HEADHUNTER

A person who finds jobs for high-paying executive positions.

The executive *headhunter* charged a hefty 25 percent of the first year's salary for executives he placed—sometimes as much as $200,000.

HISTORICAL COST

An accounting method using the original cost of an item. Compare to inflation accounting, in which the effects of inflation on an item can be shown.

Johan felt it was easiest to keep his books using the *historical cost* approach—he accounted for each item by what he paid for it originally.

HORIZONTAL ANALYSIS

A financial statement that covers more than one period, for the purpose of calculating percentage change in an account.

The newly expanded Zippy Corp. prepared a *horizontal analysis* for their stockholders so they could see how this quarter's numbers represented a huge percentage increase from last quarter's numbers.

HOUSING STARTS

A figure representing the number of new homes started in the construction field. The housing starts figure is a leading economic indicator.

New *housing starts* were up for the third consecutive quarter—an important indicator that the country is coming out of its recessionary period.

HUMAN RELATIONS

A management technique that stresses employee motivation in the workplace.

After Mr. Brown took a course in *human relations*, he made an effort to reward employees, recognize their achievements, and give incentives for good work.

HUMAN RESOURCES

A term frequently used for the personnel department.

Jack called the *human resources* department to see if they had any workers available for his job.

IDEAL CAPACITY

(see **capacity**)

IMPLIED WARRANTY

Warranty not written by the manufacturer but existing under the law.

Under an *implied warranty*, state law required that the manufacturer replace the obviously defective item.

IMPORTS

Goods that are shipped into a country for consumption.

Those televisions were *imported* from Japan; I purchased them in down-town Atlanta.

INCOME

Money received; income may be a combination of earnings and investment income.

When he'd finished filling out his tax forms, Paul saw that his *income* that year was nearly $30,000.

INDUSTRIAL

A business producing goods and services. Financial services, transportation services, and utilities are not categorized as industrial businesses. *Industrial goods* are goods used by other businesses in the production of goods and services.

Manufacturers make up one of the largest segments of the *industrial* sector in business.

The shortage of *industrial goods*, such as heavy machinery and raw materials, accounted for much of the poor output in this quarter.

INFLATION

A rise in prices.

As a result of increased consumer spending in the last year, we are experiencing a period of mild *inflation*.

IN-HOUSE

Any job done within a business, as opposed to having another company do the work.

Smithers preferred to have all the artwork done *in-house*—it was less expensive, and he certainly had enough talented people on his staff to handle it.

INSOLVENT

A state where a company is no longer able to meet its financial obligations.

After a severe drop in sales, ZYX Corp. had to declare its *insolvency* and seek protection under Chapter 11 bankruptcy.

INTEGRATION

Combining or bringing different aspects of the production process together.

As the company began to show consistently high profits, the CEO began to think about possibilities for *integration*.

Four Ways to Integrate

Forward Integration

When a company expands to do business that is closer to the consumer. When the doll manufacturer decided to buy toy retail outlets, that was an example of *forward integration*.

Backward Integration

If a company expands back toward the tools of production. When the doll manufacturer decided to buy a cotton mill for the fabric they used in production, that was an example of *backward integration*.

Horizontal Integration

If a company expands by purchasing another company that shares one stage in production. When the doll manufacturer decided to buy the action-figure manufacturer and share plastic-making facilities, that was an example of *horizontal integration*.

Vertical Integration

When a company expands by purchasing another company that shares all stages of production. When the doll manufacturer decided to purchase the mannequin company—using all its resources, from plastics to fabrics to distribution to retail—that was an example of *vertical integration*.

INVENTORY

The measure of a firm's goods, from raw materials to finished products. The two main ways of valuing inventory are first in, first out (FIFO) and last in, first out (LIFO).

XYZ Corp. preferred to use the LIFO form of *inventory* valuation so they would show lower profits this year.

JOBBER

A middleman in the sales process who buys goods from a wholesaler and sells them to a retailer.

Zippy Corp. sold to a number of *jobbers*, who purchased quantities of finished zippers from them and sold to the small retail sewing supply stores around the country.

JOURNEYMAN

A skilled worker who has successfully mastered a trade.

General Building Corp. only hired *journeymen* for their different subcontracting positions, such as plumber, carpenter, etc.

JUNIOR PARTNER

Someone who, to a limited degree, shares in the profits and decision-making of an organization.

When Brown was made a *junior partner* at LMNO after just two years, she knew that it was a matter of time before she became a full partner.

KICKBACK

An illegal payment, usually money a worker has to pay to his boss in return for employment, or an illegal bonus given to someone for securing a contract or deal.

The city inspector was fired for receiving *kickbacks* from contractors in return for giving them city contracts.

Even though Acme Corp. agreed to the union pay increase, the executives coerced their employees into giving them a *kickback* from the increased salary.

KILLING

A big profit.

Alice made a real *killing* this week, selling her stock for almost double what she'd paid for it just two months ago.

LABOR FORCE

By the U.S. Bureau of Labor Statistics definition, the labor force consists of people over the age of sixteen who are employed.

The *labor force* increased greatly the year that the first Baby Boomers hit age 16.

LADING

A shipping term referring to the actual cargo.

The bill of *lading* is a list of the contents of a package.

LAID OFF

Fired; may also be used for the positions that have been eliminated— "lay offs."

After John was *laid off* from Acme Corp., he received unemployment insurance.

Acme Corp. announced that there would be one hundred more *lay offs* before they could handle the decreased sales volume.

LAISSEZ-FAIRE

An economic theory stating that business would be better off without government interference.

The president announced a new era of *laissez-faire* economics, as the government would be deregulating business.

LAST IN, FIRST OUT (LIFO)

A method of inventory valuation.

LESS THAN CARLOAD (LTC)

A shipping term referring to the expense without the discount associated with a full carload of freight.

Because they were shipping such small amounts, Zippy Corp. had to pay the *LTC* rate.

LEVERAGE

Using borrowed money to finance elements of a business. Highly *leveraged* companies have a lot of debt in relation to the amount of their equity.

Luckily for Zippy Corp., that line of credit gave them much more *leverage* in their business deals.

LIABILITY

The money and obligations owed by a company. Liability can also be used as a legal term to refer to what extent a company is legally bound to make good a loss or damage resulting from their practice.

Acme Corp's *liabilities* were balanced out by their equity.

The lawyers for Zippy Corp. gave the bad news that the company had a great deal of *liability* for their faulty zippers.

LICENSING

Getting legal permission to use something or do something.

The owners of Acme Corp. *licensed* the use of the phrase "Acme As Always" for their toys.

LIMITED PARTNER

An investor with no liability past her investment. Limited partners generally have no say in the operation of the business.

GenCo. had a dozen or so *limited partners* to help them with financing without interfering in the day to day operation of the business.

LIQUID ASSET

Any asset in the form of cash or one that can easily be converted to cash.

XYZ had very few *liquid assets*; they weren't able to make any major purchases until they received a loan from the bank.

LOGO

A symbol phrase or representation associated with a company.

The Zippy *logo*—a silly flying zipper—had been on every package produced since the company was founded.

LOW-GRADE

Describes an item of poor quality.

Don't purchase anything from that store—they only sell *low-grade* parts.

LUMP-SUM PURCHASE

A purchase of more than one asset in a group, usually paying a discount.

The owners at XYZ Corp. were able to make a *lump-sum purchase* of a series of land parcels adjacent to their plant.

MANAGEMENT

The group of people who run a business.

When *management* and labor didn't agree on the terms of the new labor contract, labor threatened to strike.

MANUAL LABOR

Labor that involves the use of one's hands. Carpentry, assembly, and digging are examples of manual labor.

The road crews insisted that no *manual labor* be done on days when the temperature rose above 95 degrees.

MANUFACTURE

The art of making something, usually with machines and in large quantities.
"The *manufacture* of zippers is a complicated task!" cried the manager at Zippy Corp.

MARGINAL COST

The cost associated with producing one more or one less unit of an item.
The accountant of Zippy Corp. knew the *marginal cost* of each type of zipper—which were worth making more of and which were not.

MARKET
MARKET AREA

The demand for a product is also referred to as the *market*. The *market area* is the geographic description of where analysts expect demand for the product to come from.

The *market* for Zippy Zippers has increased steadily since zippered jackets came back into style. The *market area* for their sale is Atlanta—the center of the zippered-jacket phenomenon.

MARKUP

The cost difference between what a retailer pays and what it charges customers.
The *markup* on those dresses is nearly 100 percent—the store pays $50 for them and charges $95.

MENTOR

Someone who gives advice in business.
The *mentoring* program at XYZ Corp. paired new employees with veterans to help learn the business.

MERCANTILE

Anything pertaining to trade, commerce, and commercialism.
The *mercantile* agency gave out information on the credit and financial status of different companies.

MERCHANDISE

Items sold at the retail level. *Merchandising* refers to all the steps involved in selling at the retail level—purchasing, advertising, promoting, etc.
The *merchandise* at L-Mart is of the highest quality of any of the retail stores in our area.

MERGER

When two or more companies join to form one; it may or may not involve dissolution of the individual companies.
The *merger* of Zippy Corp. and Whammy Corp. would make the two relatively small companies into one powerful company to be reckoned with in their industry.

MOGUL

In the business world, a powerful and very important person.

The *moguls* from the oil cartel gathered together in the World Financial Office to discuss policies that would affect the worldwide economy.

MOM-AND-POP OPERATION

Any small, primarily family-owned company.

Even though Smith's Ice Cream Parlor had expanded from a *mom-and-pop operation* run by Mr. and Mrs. Smith into a worldwide franchise, they still had the best ice cream around.

MONOPOLY

Any market in which one company or individual controls the market and, as a result, can set the price of a good.

After Zippy and Whammy merged, they drove all their competitors out and had a *monopoly* hold on the market.

MOONLIGHTING

Holding down a second job to make extra money.

Company policy expressly forbid *moonlighting*—Zippy Corp. wanted their workers rested and ready for work each day.

NATIONAL DEBT

The money that the federal government owes, usually in the form of Treasury bills, Treasury notes, and Treasury bonds.

The interest alone on our huge *national debt* is one of the major expenses the government must pay each year.

NEGATIVE CASH FLOW

What you get when you spend more money than you receive during any period.

Although Zippy Corp. had a *negative cash flow* from a combination of major purchases for the factory and decreased sales, they felt that next year the new equipment would start paying for itself.

NET OPERATING INCOME (NOI)

Income made by a company after deducting operating expenses but before deducting income taxes and mortgage debt.

From its *net operating income*, it looked as if Zippy would do well this year, but the giant tax bill would wipe out most of their profit.

NET PRESENT VALUE (NPV)

A way of determining the value of an investment by discounting the money to be received in future years to see if that makes the investment worthy today.

Even though they could expect to make $100 more a year with the new machinery, the initial investment was too high to justify the expense after figuring out the *net present value*.

NET EARNINGS

The money made after deducting all expenses and taxes from gross earnings.

Jay's *net earnings* were considerably less than his gross earnings because his overhead was so high.

NETWORKING

Meeting, greeting, and shaking hands; networking involves making and using professional contacts to get work.

Popular in the 1980s were *networking* parties, where business people would swap their cards and make deals.

NET WORTH

All a company's or individual's assets minus its liabilities.

The *net worth* of CompCorp. was quite substantial after they paid off some of their larger loans.

NONPROFIT ORGANIZATION

A company that doesn't pay taxes. Nonprofits—things like churches, hospitals, and charities—may also receive tax deductible contributions.

When you purchase something for a *nonprofit organization*, you don't need to pay sales tax on that item.

NOTARY PUBLIC

A person who is authorized by the government to take affidavits and acknowledgments, called "notarizing."

Before she signed that legal document, Jan had to find a *notary public* to *notarize* her signature so that it would stand up in court.

OCEAN BILL OF LADING (OBI)

The bill of lading that covers a package from port to port.

Before the ship departed, Ship Corp. checked that all the *ocean bills of lading* were attached to all the packages in their cargo.

OFF THE BOOKS

An expense or payment that is not formally recorded. A transaction that is off the books is usually hidden from taxation.

Marvin was willing to take such low pay because he would be paid *off the books,* and therefore wouldn't pay any income taxes on the amount.

OLIGOPOLY

A market characterized by a few large producers.

"If only I wasn't dealing with a damn oligopoly," said Flanders, "I'd take my business elsewhere. Unfortunately, I've already got burned by Flamethrowerland's other two competitors, Fire Me Up and Burning Down The House."

OPERATING EXPENSES

Expenses a company incurs to keep production of goods and services going.

Although the electric bill and property taxes were included in the monthly *operating expenses*, income tax and asset depreciation were not.

ORAL CONTRACT

A contract that is not in writing. Oral contracts, usually consisting of a spoken agreement, may be enforceable in court.

Marie felt that she had gotten an *oral contract* with Zippy Corp. when the vice president assured her that she would supply all the fabric for their new zipper model.

OUTLET

A retail store that is operated by a manufacturer. Outlet stores are usually for the purpose of selling off overstock and irregular or damaged goods.

The Cougats always made a yearly trek to the *outlets* to get the best bargain on school clothes and supplies.

OVERAGE

Having too much of a supply. Overage may also refer to a provision in some leases to collect a certain percentage of a retail store's sales above the rental.

There was an *overage* of sheet metal this month so next month's supply had to be adjusted.

There wouldn't be any *overage* this month because sales at Q-Mart were horrendous.

PADDING

Adding unnecessary or irrelevant material.

Jones was fired for constantly *padding* his hours on his time sheet; he frequently billed the company for time he hadn't really spent working.

Parker was always *padding* her expense account, adding a dinner bill that wasn't work related, for example.

"This report is nothing but *padding*!" yelled the customer. "You added five pages of description that were not needed to make your point."

PARTNERSHIP

When two or more people join to form a business. Limited partners will contribute only money, not input or expertise. General partners, however, share all responsibilities.

"Hey, you've got the people skills and I know accounting. Let's form a *partnership* and start our dream business together," suggested Brown.

PATENT

Legal right to hold sole ownership of an invention for a period of time. If someone uses that invention without authorization, he can be charged with *patent infringement*.

Green was awfully glad she'd gotten a *patent* on her new space-age pen—every company in the state was clamoring to buy the rights to make it.

PAYABLES

(see **accounts payable**)

PAYLOAD

Any cargo, or part of a cargo, that will produce income. Payload is typically expressed in weight.

That shipment of peaches was 200 pounds of *payload* for the peach growers.

PAYROLL

The total of all the paychecks paid out to a company's employees.

After they expanded to 2,000 employees, XYZ Corp. hired an independent company to do *payroll* for them. The job of writing out all those checks and keeping track of employees was too much for the accounting department.

PER CAPITA

Per person. A *per capita* expense is one that a company has to pay for each person it employs.

Instituting this new health plan would incur a *per capita* expense of $300.

PER DIEM

Per day. Expense accounts in business are often calculated *per diem*, meaning that an employee is given a daily allowance for her expenses.

Before Brown went on his business trip, the company cut him a check for $700, a *per diem* allowance of $100 for each of the seven days he'd be gone.

PERQUISITE OR "PERK"

Any fun stuff your company offers in addition to salary. Also called fringe benefits.

The salary wasn't great a Zippy Corp., but the *perks*—from a full health plan, retirement plan, and company car to a lifetime supply of zippers—were great.

PETER PRINCIPLE

A theory that people in a company will be promoted until they reach a job at which they are incompetent. The end result is a lot of people who don't do their jobs well.

Just because Mr. Green excelled at all the bookkeeping jobs he'd had didn't make him a good chief of the department—a perfect example of the *Peter principle* at work.

PIECE WORK

Work that is paid for per piece. Piece work is often sent in by independent workers, called *piece workers*.

Acme Corp. had all their new line of slimeball covers sewn by *piece workers* in the area at 2 cents per piece.

PINK SLIP

Often notices of termination of employment are written on pink slips of paper. When a company is sending out *pink slips*, it is firing employees. May also be used as a verb, as in "Jones was *pink slipped* on Friday."

The cutbacks at Zippy Corp. led to the issue of 300 *pink slips* last week; they had to let a substantial part of their work force go.

POINT OF PURCHASE DISPLAY (POP)
POINT OF PURCHASE SALE

Point of purchase displays are those sales displays that sit on or next to the counter where you make your purchase; they rely on impulse, or un-planned, purchases. Any sale made at the *point of purchase* is called a *point of purchase sale.*

Zippy paid a premium to its retailers to put its new zippers in a fancy *point of purchase display.* These new, low-priced zippers were often picked up last minute by shoppers waiting for their credit cards to receive approval.

PREMIUM

An additional amount paid above the value market.

That figure represents a *premium* over recent market sales, due to the great demand.

PROFIT

The difference between what it cost to produce something and what is received for selling it.

They made a 300% *profit* on that item—it cost only one dollar to produce and yet it sold for four dollars.

QUALITY CONTROL

Any process a company uses to ensure that their product has a con-sistently high quality. Inspections and consumer feedback are some quality control tools.

After instituting a whole program of *quality control*—from spot-check inspections to new computer evaluation programs—Zippy Corp. was able to lower the number of defective zippers produced.

QUOTA

A specific mark that a department tries to meet. A quota may either be a number of items a department wants to make or sell, or a certain increase over the last period.

All the departments met their monthly *quotas* of selling 10 percent more than the previous month.

REAL INCOME

An income as it reflects purchasing power.

When prices rose 10 percent that year, Smithers informed his boss that he wanted a 10 percent raise so that his *real income* would remain the same.

REBATE

Money that is refunded to the purchaser of a product from the manufacturer. Rebates are often given as incentives to buy.

LawnMan offers a $20 rebate on lawnmowers. Even though they cost nearly $300, with the sale at the hardware store and the $20 you'll get back after mailing in your rebate form, it will be worth it.

RED TAPE

Needed paperwork to accomplish a task.

The new government agency was attempting to cut down on beaurocratic *red tape;* you only needed to fill out a short one-page application to get your loan.

REQUISITION

A form filled out to request something.

Brown filled out a purchase *requisition* for 200 notebooks and sent it to the stock department.

RESEARCH AND DEVELOPMENT (R&D)

The department responsible for creating new products and doing the research for marketing and manufacturing needs.

Zippy Corp's *R&D* department came up with a full marketing proposal for the newly developed Spiffy Zipper.

RESIDUAL VALUE

An asset's remaining value after it has been fully depreciated.

The *residual value* of that machinery was so low, it wasn't even worth it to try to sell it.

RETAIL

Goods and services sold directly to the consumer. Retail items are usually sold in smaller quantities than wholesale purchases.

"Never buy *retail!*" said the ad claiming to offer wholesale prices to consumers who were willing to purchase items in bulk amounts.

RETURNS

Items that are brought back to a store for either credit or exchange.

Green receives a profit from the sales we make, less the *returns*.

REVENUE

Income from an investment or salary. Revenue also refers to the taxes that the government collects.

The increases in *revenue* at XYZ Corp. were directly attributed to a more efficient management.

The *revenue* raised by the increase in taxes was enough to pay for some of the government's new programs.

SALE

Any receipt of cash in exchange for goods or services. A sale may also refer to a discount.

L-Mart made over 2,000 *sales* that weekend because of the big *sale* they were having—20 percent off every price in the store.

SCALAGE

A deduction given for an item that is likely to shrink or leak during shipping.

There would be a 2 percent *scalage* discount for the grain shipment.

SEMIVARIABLE COSTS

Costs that vary with production amounts, but not proportionately.

Our utilities are a *semivariable cost*—if we produce less, we use less electricity, but not a lot less; we run machines less often, but the lights and computers are still running.

SENIORITY

How long a person has been employed by a company.

He had the benefits of *seniority*—he'd been in the firm longer than anyone else.

SERVICE

The intangible thing a business might sell, such as assistance, consultation and advice. Service also refers to the help a manufacturer gives to a purchaser after the product is brought home.

XYZ Corp. also offered a consultation *service* for its clients—it would conduct market research and offer strategies.

Mike had to call the manufacturer for *service* when his new dishwasher broke down.

SEVERANCE PAY

Pay offered to an employee after he or she has been fired.

Zippy Corp. had to let some employees go, but it offered them a generous *severance pay* of one week's salary for each year they had been with the company.

SHAKEUP

A major change in organization, employment and/or structure at a company.

After a disastrous year, there was a major *shakeup* at Acme Corp.—all the offices were reorganized and a new CEO was hired.

SHRINKAGE

The difference between what you actually have and what you should have. Shrinkage occurs in inventory if items are missing, lost, or unaccounted for. Shrinkage occurs during shipping if an item settles or leaks.

The accountants at Zippy Corp. were happy after inventory had been completed—they had less than 1 percent *shrinkage*.

Expect some *shrinkage* during shipping; contents of the bin may leak.

SLOWDOWN
When employees at a plant purposely slow down production; usually used as a protest.

Although they did not strike, employees at Acme Corp. instituted a *slowdown* to protest the measly wage increases offered in the new contract.

SOFT MARKET
A market characterized by oversupply of an item.

Due to an excess of zippers this year, it was a *soft market*.

SPECIALTY SHOP
Any retailer that sells a small range of types of items, or items that focus on one general theme.

That mall had only small *specialty shops* in it, stores such as Light Bulbs R Us, Only Jeans, and House of Zippers.

SPILLOVER
Any effect, negative or positive, a business has on its neighbors.

The horrible noise from the zipper plant had a negative *spillover* on the neighboring community.

The activity brought into town by the new retail outlet had a positive *spillover* to the other smaller retail shops in the area.

STRIKE
A complete stop to work as a protest. Strikes are used as a final bargaining tool when contracts are being negotiated.

When the workers and management could not reach a settlement on cost of living increases, workers had no choice but to go out on *strike*.

TAKEOVER
When a company changes hands. A takeover may be friendly, if management wants to be sold, or unfriendly, if management fought against the takeover.

The sharks at LMNO Corp. started an unfriendly *takeover* of QRST Corp.

TARGET MARKET
The group of people who generally buy the type of product being marketed.

The researchers at Market Corp. told the manufacturers of the new Quik Zip Zipper that their *target market* was women between the ages of thirty-five and fifty, and that's where they should gear their advertisements.

TASK FORCE
A team formed with the express purpose of completing a specific task.

The CEO of Acme Corp. appointed a *task force* to investigate the decline in sales from the last two quarters.

TELEMARKETING
Selling and gathering information about products by telephone.

After they did a direct mail solicitation, Zippy Corp. followed up with a *telemarketing* campaign to all the people who'd received flyers to see if any wished to place an order.

TIP

Money a customer pays directly to a company employee as a reward for good service. Also called a *gratuity*.

An old story has it that he term *tip* comes from colonial days when tavern keepers would ask for additional donations for the waiters and waitresses in a bowl marked "To Insure Promptness."

TRADE

Any business or profession may be called a trade, but the term most often refers to a skilled worker.

The carpenter learned his *trade* from his father and grandfather.

TRADE PUBLICATION

Any newspaper or magazine specifically devoted to one profession.

Whenever he was looking for work, Jones checked the *trade publications* first; they listed only jobs in his field.

TRADE SHOW

A large show, usually in a hall or convention center, in which different companies within a certain general trade exhibit products and services and make sales to retailers.

Tweezerman had an exhibit of its new line of high quality tweezers and beauty supplies in the beauty *trade show*.

UNDEREMPLOYED

Being employed at a level below one's education and training.

After Dr. Bob lost his professorship for sleeping with a student, he found himself *underemployed* at a burger stand.

UNEMPLOYMENT

Having no work, but being able and willing to work.

The new *unemployment* figures were at an all-time low—a great number of people who were willing and able to work were gainfully employed.

UNFAIR COMPETITION

Utilizing misleading advertising or packaging to lead a purchaser to believe that he is buying a different manufacturer's product.

The manufacturers of that soda Pipsi Kola were accused of *unfair competition*; their name and logo were so similar to Pepsi Cola that they were obviously trying to mislead consumers.

UNION

An organization authorized by employees of a certain trade to look out for employee benefits. Unions may negotiate contracts or call for employee strikes.

The AFL-CIO is the largest *union* in the United States, representing employees from many different trades.

UNITED PARCEL SERVICE (UPS)

A private freight delivery service.

When Jane wanted to ship some of the new line of zippers to her aunt, she called *UPS* to deliver the package.

UNSKILLED LABOR

Labor that requires no special skill and can be easily replaced.

The *unskilled labor* in that factory will soon be largely replaced by robotics on the assembly line.

VARIABLE COSTS

Any cost that changes proportionately in relation to output.

Variable costs, such as materials used for production, were the easiest to adjust when Acme Corp. had to cut back.

VOUCHER

A slip of paper that gives authorization to pay.

Brown sent his signed expense *voucher* to accounting so he would be reimbursed for his costs on his next paycheck.

WAGES

Pay. Minimum wage set by union and federal legislation is called the *wage floor.* If wages will not be increased for a set period, that is called a *wage freeze.*

The president asked for a minimum *wage* increase to five dollars per hour.

Management called for a one year *wage freeze,* due to the recessionary period they were going through.

WAYBILL

A paper used in shipping that states the route the cargo will take and all the shipping costs.

The shipper checked the *waybill* on the packages before he loaded his truck.

WHOLESALE PRICES

Lower prices, generally associated with buying large bulk quantities of an item.

The appeal of those large food stores is that they are able to offer *wholesale prices* on bulk purchases.

WHOLESALER

A person who buys in large quantity at a discount from a manufacturer and sells to a retailer.

The *wholesaler* stocked up in his warehouse for shipment to smaller retailers around the country.

Chapter 2

COMPUTERS

"The computer is no better than its programs."
—Elting Elmore Morison

ADDRESS

In the on-line world, whether it be a large commercial service like America Online, or the giant Internet, an address means an electronic address, not your street address. All addresses follow a similar pattern: a person's screen name (also called a user id), followed by @, followed by a domain name.

The *address* for the president is President@Whitehouse.gov.

When someone says an address out loud, it is read in a specific way. You would say "at" for the @ sign, and "dot" for any periods. For example:

Lizb@panix.com

is said:

"Liz B at panix dot com"

AMERICA ONLINE (AOL)

America Online is one of the "big three" commercial online services. Think of it as one of the major cable networks. You pay a monthly fee for access to all the services on America Online. America Online is typically referred to as AOL (spoken as separate letters, like HBO).

Margie joined *AOL* so that she could have access to daily weather reports for her school project.

ANONYMOUS FTP

(see **FTP**)

APPLICATION

Another word for a type of program. There are spreadsheet applications, graphics applications, word processing applications, and database applications.

Microsoft Word is a type of word processing *application*.

ARCHIE

Archie is a program used on the Internet to search for information locations. Think of Archie as a catalog for anonymous FTP sites—type in the name of a file or directory you need, and Archie will search through its files and give you the name of the host where it is located. You can telnet to an Archie server and ask it to search for you.

Lee typed "telnet archie.funet.fi" to reach the *Archie* site in Finland.

Public Archie Sites

You can go to a different country to search the archie archives for that country.

Austria   archie.edvz.uni-linz.ac.at
Australia   archie.au
Canada   archie.uqam.ca
England   archie.doc.ic.ac.uk
Germany   archie.th-darmstadt.de
Israel   archie.cs.huji.ac.li
Italy   archie.unipi.it
Japan   archie.kuis.kyoto-u.ac.jp
Korea   archie.kr
NewZealand   archie.nz
SouthKorea   archie.sogang.ac.kr
Spain   archie.rediris.ed
Sweden   archie.luth.se
Switzerland   archie.switch.ch
Taiwan   archie.ncu.edu.tw
NewYork   archie.ans.net
NewJersey   archie.internic.net
Nebraska   archie.unl.edu

ARCHIVE

A group of files stored together.

Louise downloaded all the files as a single *archive*.

ARCHIVE SITE

A machine that provides access to a collection of files across the Internet.

The anonymous FTP *archive site* allowed Mario to access a range of material through the FTP protocol.

ASCII

A text-only file; in other words, no formatting (such as bullets) or fancy pictures. ASCII (pronounced ASK-ee) files can be used from computer to computer because the basic text is the same from program to program.

If you want to send a Word for Windows file to someone without Windows, you can save it as MS-DOS text and it will be converted to *ASCII* format.

ATTRIBUTES

A file's special features; for example, a file may be a read-only file (meaning you cannot do anything to it other than read it). You can say it has a read-only attribute.

Attribute is also another name used for the fields in a database.

In a database, the tables are divided into rows and fields, which are also called *attributes*.

AUXILIARY STORAGE

Where data and programs are stored when they are not being used—sort of like a really expensive file cabinet.

Auxiliary storage is nonvolatile, meaning that the stuff packed away in there will not be lost when the power is turned off.

BACKSLASH

(\) is a backslash. It is not found on a conventional typewriter's keyboard, only on a computer keyboard. Don't confuse it with a regular (/) slash.

BACKUP

A copy of your original file made in case anything happens to that original file. May be used as a verb:

The supervisor advised his crew to *back up* their files during the storm.

Or a noun:

I'm so glad I made a *backup* of that file—that lightning bolt screwed up my hard drive.

BASIC INPUT/OUTPUT SYSTEM (BIOS)

The basic control commands for the computer.

The *BIOS* gives basic instruction to the operating system regarding the keyboard, monitors and disk drives.

BAUD RATE

The baud rate of a modem refers to the bits per second (bps) that can speed through the phone line. The higher the number, the faster you can transfer data. Typical baud rates are 2,400, 9,600, 14,400 and 28,800.

I refuse to get a modem with a *baud rate* of less than 14,400—the phone charges are too high with the lower-speed modems.

BETA PROGRAMS

A program being tested before its official release. It may contain some bugs, which is why it is released as a beta.

Use that *beta* version at your own risk.

BINARY

A number system that uses only two digits—0 and 1.

BITNET

A worldwide network similar to but separate from the Internet.

Bitnet, begun in 1981 at the City University of New York, stands for "Because It's Time Network."

BITS

A single switch inside the computer which has a value of either 0 or 1, millions of which form the basis for memory in a PC.

A group of eight *bits* is called a byte.

BITS PER SECOND (BPS)

(see **baud rate**)

BOOT

When you turn on your computer, it will boot or load up the operating system it has stored in its memory. If you hit the reset button, you are rebooting, or giving your system a warm boot.

When the screen froze, Jan had to *reboot* to get the system moving again.

BROWSER

You need a browser to navigate your way through a hypertext document. In the Internet, World Wide Web may lead you through different types of resources (newsgroups, gopher, telnet, etc). A browser is the tool you need to move seamlessly from one type of document to another.

The WWW *browser* initiated a telnet session during my search.

BUFFER

A spot in a PC's memory that stores something you just used or are about to use.

BULLETIN BOARD SYSTEMS (BBS)

A bulletin board system—commonly called a BBS—is a collection of message boards and files devoted to a particular topic. Many are maintained by individuals or organizations. Some require a fee to use; others are free. There are a few on the Internet, but most may be dialed directly. A BBS is more like your community newspaper than a commercial online system.

I uploaded a wonderful article the other day from the *Hacker's World BBS*.

BYTE

A group of eight bits; bytes are used as a measure of your computer's capacity, usually seen as kilobytes or megabytes.

I just got the latest PC, with 500 *kilobytes* of space.

CAPACITY

The number of bytes that can be stored in memory. This number is usually expressed as kilobytes, megabytes, or the wholly impressive and somewhat scary-sounding gigabyte.

I have to get a new computer with more *capacity*—the games I play have taken up all the space I have.

CASE

Refers to letter as being either uppercase (ABCDE) or lowercase (abcde). Some programs are case sensitive, meaning that a command of "D" will be different than a command of "d." If a program is not case sensitive, then you may type in capital letters or lower case without affecting the operations.

On many of the commercial online services, commands are not *case sensitive*.

CELL

In a database, the little rectangle where a row and column intersect.
The table had twenty cells, consisting of four rows and five columns.

CENTRAL PROCESSING UNIT (CPU)

The computer's brain or microprocessor.
As technology develops, manufacturers are finding ways to make the *CPU* faster and faster.

CHAT

If you are online you may be able to find a chat facility or a "chat room." Here, you can enter into a "conversation" with one or more people who may be present at the same place at the same time. This involves typing a message and entering it so it is displayed and waiting for other people to type in a response. Some are hosted and revolve around a topic ("The New Tax Increase"); others are more free-form.

Armand engaged in an interesting debate about censorship in an AOL *chat* room.

Don't Be a Pita—Chat Acronyms

AFK	Away from keyboard
BAK	Back at keyboard
BRB	Be right back
BTW	By the way
LOL	Laughing out loud
L8R	Later
OIC	Oh, I see
OMG	Oh, my God!
GMTA	Great minds think alike
IMHO	In my honest opinion
LTNS	Long time no see
PITA	Pain in the ass
ReHi	Hi again
ROTFL	Rolling on the floor laughing
RTFM	Read the f***ing manual
WRT	With respect to
:::POOF:::	Signing off now

CD-ROM

Compact Disk-Read Only Memory; a CD-ROM for your computer requires a special drive. The CDs you purchase look just like audio CDs, only they store all sorts of stuff, from games to whole encyclopedias (complete with audio and video clips). What's that Read Only Memory part? Well, unlike regular programs, you cannot write on or modify a CD-ROM.
My favorite *CD-ROM* game is called *Doom*.

CLARINET

A service of newsgroups. To get Clarinet on your server, you must pay for it, and unlike a Usenet newsgroup, you may generally just read entries, not post to them.

Clarinet newsgroups are real news, they come from sources such as UPI.

CLICK

Pressing down on that little button on the mouse; often a double click is required (which means press twice on the button).

Double *click* on the icon to open that program.

CLIENT SERVERS

Networks of PCs linked together by powerful server computers.

Large companies are increasingly relying on *client servers* rather than the older, more costly systems that relied on mainframe computers.

CLOCK SPEED

The measure of how fast a computer can think, measured in megahertz (MHz). A computer with 66 *MHz* will think faster than one with a clock speed of 33 *MHz*.

CLONE

A copy of an original; most PCs are IBM clones—copies of the type of computer that IBM makes and compatible with all the software that an IBM computer can use.

I wanted an IBM *clone* so I could use all the software I already had with my old IBM.

COMPRESSED FILES

When large files are stored, they may be compressed, or made smaller, to take up less space. When downloading, a compressed file will take less time. After a file has been downloaded, it must be uncompressed.

Often when a file is *compressed*, it will have some letters added to its file name. For example, a document titled BOOK may be retitled BOOK.Z when it is *compressed*.

COMPUTER SIMULATION

Any activity that is not really taking place but simulated by a computer program.

The pilots used *computer simulation* to give them practice with different emergency situations before they climbed into the cockpit of a real plane.

COMPUSERVE

One of the "big three" commercial online services; CompuServe is generally considered to the best service for business users.

CompuServe offers basic services and many extended services, like games.

COMPATIBLE

A computer that can run DOS software; this used to be something to worry about, but today most PCs are *compatible*.

CONSOLE DEVICE

A keyboard and computer monitor. Don't use this term—it's pretty nerdy. "Have you seen my new *console device*?" smirked the computer technician.

CONVENTIONAL MEMORY

The memory DOS uses to run a program.
Conventional memory is sometimes called DOS memory or low-DOS memory.

CURSOR

The blinking line on the screen that shows position; the cursor shows where the next thing typed will land.
The *cursor* is controlled by the *cursor* keys—the left, right, up, and down arrows, and the Page Up, Page Down, Home, and End keys.

CYBERSPACE

A term, first used by the science fiction writer William Gibson, that refers to a network of computers, such as the Internet.
If you go online, you are wandering around in *cyberspace*.

DATA

Any information gathered.
The *data* revealed that most people are clueless about how a computer works.

DATABASE

A collection of information grouped by common characteristics. An address book is a personal database. There are many different types of database programs available for the computer.
John customized the business *database* to contain information about all his vendors and their orders.

DEBUGGING

Locating and correcting program errors.
The recall of all those beta programs was necessary until they were *debugged*.

DEFAULT SETTING

What the computer will do unless told otherwise; the default setting is the standard in that category.
Elaine had to change her *default* port *settings* after she reconfigured her computer.

DESKTOP PUBLISHING

Producing professional-looking documents using software to combine graphics and text.
Juanita, president of the Bobby Sherman Fan Club, was able to put out her own newsletter with her *desktop publishing* program.

DIRECTORY

A collection of files; there are main directories (sometimes called root directories) and subdirectories.

To view the *directory*, type DIR at the prompt.

DISK OPERATING SYSTEM (DOS)

The main program that runs a PC and all its programs.

Jane installed the latest version of *DOS* on her PC to run Windows.

DISK

Two types of disks—hard disks and floppies—are used to store information. Floppy disks are the ones you can pop in and out (they aren't always so floppy) and hard disks are the ones inside your computer that cannot be removed.

The "c" drive is where my hard *disk* is located.

DISKETTE

Although it is perfectly OK to use the term disk to refer to a floppy, some people prefer the term diskette, to distinguish them from hard disks.

A package of ten *diskettes* is on sale at Radio Shack this week.

DOMAIN

In a database, the name of a field or attribute. In cyberspace, a domain is the part of an address following the @ sign.

In the e-mail address Lorenzo.tpr@review.com, the "review.com" part is the *domain*.

DOWNLINK

In satellite communications, the link from the satellite to the ground.

The technicians felt that the communications were not going through due to a problem with the *downlink*.

DOWNLOAD

The process of transferring data or programs from a communications network to a personal computer.

David *downloaded* the newest version of the game DISGUSTO from the Prodigy game files.

E-MAIL

Electronic mail and the software that supports it; e-mail can be sent within a company, via a commercial online service, or through the Internet.

She *e-mailed* him with the information about the new meeting and time, as he needed the information immediately.

EMOTICONS

Icons made to give a visual cue for e-mails or postings in cyberspace. Two of the most common are the smiley face :-) and the sad face :-(. You can often get the idea by looking at them sideways.

ERGONOMICS

The study of design and arrangement of equipment so that it can be used comfortably and efficiently.

The new *ergonomically*-designed keyboard was designed to reduce the occurrence of carpal-tunnel syndrome, which was affecting many of the office workers.

ESCAPE

A key on a computer keyboard, typically marked "Esc." In many programs, it allows you to cancel a command or quit the program.

"Hit the *escape* key to exit back to DOS," the computer screen read.

EXPANDED MEMORY

Extra memory, useful to DOS and many DOS applications.

Chris decided it was a good idea to buy an *expanded memory* program for his PC.

FREQUENTLY ASKED QUESTIONS (FAQ)

As you start out in the Internet, you will have many, many questions. The thing is, a lot of other people have the same questions. You may see a posting in many newsgroups marked FAQ for frequently asked questions. It is always a good idea to check out this first to make sure you don't post a question that someone has already taken the trouble to answer for you. If you participate in an ongoing discussion you will find that not having to address the same questions over and over again is really helpful.

A typical *FAQ* in the Disney newsgroups is, "Is it true that Walt Disney is cryogenically frozen?"

FACSIMILE OR FAX

A machine capable of transmitting an image of a document or picture over telephone lines.

"*Fax* resumes to our offices and we will contact your for an appointment," read the classified ad.

FIELD

In a database, each separate space that data is broken into, is called a field. In a simple address book, you might have the following fields:

Last Name
First Name
Street Address
City
State
Zip Code
Telephone Number

FILE

A collection of data; the contents of a disk file are just like those in a file cabinet and can be filled with just about anything: a word processing document, a group of spreadsheets, and so on.

The disk marked "Meetings 1995" had the *files* for all the minutes of the meeting held in that year.

FILE TRANSFER PROTOCOL (FTP)

Allows files to be transferred from one computer to another on the Internet.

One of the most frequently used services on the Internet is the anonymous *FTP*. Using this, you may copy files from thousands of different computers around the world.

Internet Tip

Archie will search the FTP database to help you find the host and file you may be looking for.

FINGER

A service to help find out more about an Internet user, perhaps his or her name and other personal information about the person. A university professor may post his schedule for his students to find. Sometimes you can use finger to find out information about a place (schedule, weather).

Finger may also be used as an adjective:

The *finger* system will tell you that user's phone number.

Or as a verb:

"Why don't we *finger* that use rid to find out who she really is?"

FLAME

The online equivalent of a hissy fit. Flaming occurs if someone posts what someone else thinks is a stupid comment, or if someone takes offense at someone else. Flames can be very nasty and may escalate to flame wars, which, like any spat, may be boring or fun to watch (and read), depending on the creativity of the venom.

"I'm new to this forum, so don't *flame* me," pleaded the post.

FLOPPY DISK

(see **disk**)

FONT

A typeface or style of text. Many word processing programs come with a variety of fonts, so you can print in lots of funny ways.

> ### Some Fun Fonts
> This is called Linotext Font.
> This is called Bauhaus Light Font.
> This is called Brush Script Font.

FORMAT

To use a disk with a DOS program, it must be formatted. This process prepares it for storing files and information. Many *floppies* can be purchased preformatted, so nothing need be done before information is stored.

Jan *formatted* the disk before she copied the files onto it.

GIGABYTE

A billion bytes. (Wow. Sort of awes you, doesn't it?) May be abbreviated as 1,000 MB (megabytes).

I just updated my hard drive to one with a *gigabyte* of memory—I'm sure I'll have enough room to hold all that programming and more.

GOPHER

A gopher will give you a series of menus for local providers to help you access different text information.

There are many different *gopher* systems on the Internet, and most will connect to others so that if you are connected to a *gopher* in, say, Illinois, it will connect to a foreign *gopher* site for you.

GRAPHICS

Information presented as a graph or a chart; more generally, pictures.

He appreciated the *graphics* in her presentation; they made the drop in prices over the last year look so much more dramatic.

GRAPHICS INTERCHANGE FORMAT (GIF)

Pictures must be stored in specific types of files. One of the most popular types is the Graphics Interchange Format, or GIF file, recognized by the extension .gif. You need a GIF viewer to see the picture in the GIF file. Many of the most popular downloads online are GIF files, and lots and lots of them are erotica, although you may certainly find a picture of Peter Jennings, if that's your thing.

HACKER

One who illegally gains access to a private database.

Hackers got into the school records database and changed all their grades from Cs to As.

HARD COPY

The fancy name for a printed-out page.

Did you make a *hard copy* of that document to hand out in class this week?

HARD DISK

The long-term, main storage device for your computer.
What's the capacity of that *hard disk*?

HARDWARE

In the computer world, there's hardware and there's software: hardware refers to the mechanical computer object; software is the programming. Software runs on hardware.

She knew from the way the computer responded that it was a *hardware* problem; the word-processing program worked well on the other terminal.

HAYES-COMPATIBLE

The original modem was a Hayes micromodem; most communications software works with a Hayes-compatible modem.

The default setting was for a *Hayes-compatible* modem.

HOST

Any computer system with a distinct address.

Each *host* on the Internet has a name and a numeric network address called its IP address.

HYPERTEXT

Data that contains links to other pieces of data; a hypertext document may have highlighted words, which if clicked on will send you to a dictionary definition. Think of hypertext as layered documents with little pathways that lead you from one to another.

A card catalog is a *hypertext* instrument, since—if you look up *Romeo and Juliet*—it will send you over to Shakespeare as well.

I/O

Input/Output—the way a computer works—you put stuff in and it puts it out.

ICON

Little pictures or symbols that are used in place of words or commands. Click on the icons to open different programs—so much more fun than in DOS, where you have to type in a command.

My favorite *icon* is the one for Quicken—a big dollar sign with the logo across it.

INFORMATION HIGHWAY

Otherwise known as the electronic highway or cyberspace; just another name for the Internet.

Vice President Al Gore urged all Americans to learn about the *information highway*.

INTEGRITY

Usually used to refer to a system or its data. Integrity generally refers to quality, accuracy, reliability, and timeliness.

System *integrity* was violated due to error.

INTERNET

A worldwide network of computer networks. It all began as a network of computers for the United States Defense Department called the Defense Advanced Research Projects Agency Network (DARPANET). It has since expanded to a wholly ungovernmental, ungovernable network of networks, not managed by any one group. It is the source of an almost unimaginable amount of information.

My *Internet* account allows me access to thousands of usegroups, files at many universities, and even video clips from the latest movies.

INTERNET RELAY CHAT (IRC)

A talk facility that allows more than one user to participate at a time. You can enter into a party line of sorts (usually arranged around a specific subject) and join in or just "listen" in by watching the typed communications on the screen. This is the Internet version of a chat room.

JUGHEAD

Jughead will search Gopher menus to help you start your search.

Veronica and *Jughead* are two tools that keep track of Gopher menus around the world.

KEYBOARD

The part of your computer that looks like a typewriter is called the keyboard.

Vic got a new ergonomic *keyboard* especially designed to reduce wrist strain.

KILOBYTE (KB)

One thousand bytes.

The computer had storage space of 300 *KB*.

LAPTOP

A really small computer which, as you may have guessed, can fit on a lap and be carried around.

As Michele took her seat on Transcontinental Flight 405, she found herself surrounded by a sea of *laptop* computers, each perched on a tray table.

LETTER-QUALITY

A description of a printed page that is good enough to send out as a business letter.

One of the great advantages of the ink-jet printers over the dot-matrix printers is that they are able to produce *letter-quality* products.

LISTSERV

Many mailing lists on the Internet are administered by a special program called a listserv.

An address that starts with the name *listserv* is from a mailing list that is administered by a *listserv* program rather than manually.

LIQUID CRYSTAL DISPLAY (LCD)

A type of computer screen, especially used on many laptops, which is limited to black-and-white type display.

His old *LCD* monitor wouldn't dipole the color graphics from the presentation.

LOAD

To put something from a disk onto a computer's memory.

I just *loaded* that new version of *Doom* on my computer—let's play it!

LOCAL AREA NETWORK (LAN)

A group of computers connected directly to each other by cable.

The philosophy department has its own *LAN*, which is hooked up to other departments by a WAN.

MACRO

A program inside a regular program, designed to carry out a specific command or function. A macro can automate a boring, repetitive task so you don't need to go through all the steps each time.

In DOS, *macros* are referred to as batch files.

MAGNETIC INK CHARACTER RECOGNITION (MICR)

A machine-readable code used in the banking industry. Those funky numbers at the bottom of your check are read by machines and tell where the check is going and from whence it came.

All banks in the United States and some banks in many foreign countries use *MICR* readers to process their checks.

MAILING LIST

On the Internet, subscribing to a mailing list means getting lots of e-mail about a certain topic. Some mailing lists are just like newsgroups, only they come right to your mailbox. Some are moderated, meaning that someone out there decided which posts to send out to which members.

Subscribing to a few *mailing lists* is a sure way to have a full mailbox every day.

MAINFRAMES

A large, very powerful system capable of serving more than one user at the same time.

Mainframe computers often require a special environment and flooring to accommodate them.

MEGABYTE (M, MB)

One million bytes; also called "megs." Impressive, but not as impressive as a gigabyte.

My new hard drive has 500 *MB* of storage space.

MEGAHERTZ (MHZ)

The measurement of speed of a system clock. Each megahertz is equal to about a million cycles per second.

Their latest PC had a 33 *MHz* speed.

MEMORY

Where a computer stores the information it is processing. Memory is a temporary place—think of it as your kitchen counter: you keep things there temporarily (we hope) while you're working on them. Memory is usually in the form of RAM chips.

I need more *memory* in my computer—it can't handle tasks quickly enough.

MENU

Lists of commands, options, whatever. In some programs, a menu will drop down after you've clicked on a word or icon; in other programs, you'll need to type in a command or strike a key to get a menu.

I clicked on "Save" in the file *menu*.

MICROCOMPUTERS

A personal desktop computer. Since IBM came along, microcomputers are now referred to as PCs.

The IBM *microcomputer* and all its clones became commonly known as PCs.

MICROPROCESSORS

Also called the CPU, or the processor; the brain of the computer. CPUs are given names such as 286, 386, 486, and Pentium, which refer to how quickly the brain can think.

I updated my old 286 *microprocessor* to a 486—my applications move four times as fast as before.

MODEM

A device used to transmit data over a telephone line by turning it into signals. You need a modem to go online. Some modems are external, hooking up outside your computer, and some are internal, or hooked inside your computer where you can't see them.

The word *modem* is a contraction of the words modulator-demodulator.

MONITOR

The screen.

My new *monitor* is a SVGA—I can run all sorts of special CD-ROM programs.

Faster Than a Speeding Bullet It's SVGA
CGAColor Graphics Adapter

The first video system that offered both color text and graphics. It was soon replaced by **EGAEnhanced Graphics Adapter**; many more colors than the CGA, plus text that was easier to read. Soon, however, it was toppled by **VGAVideo Graphic Array**; great graphics, high resolution, superior text. It, however, was topped by the **SVGASuper Video Graphics Array**; like the VGA, only better. Many of the super–graphic CD-ROM titles need **SVGA** to run.

MOSAIC

Mosaic is a type of browser, which has its own graphics and allows you to launch multimedia applications.

If you are really into the World Wide Web, installing *Mosaic* is a way to help you enjoy all its features even more.

MOTHERBOARD

The main circuitry board of a computer. It houses the CPU, the memory, and all that stuff you may not want to think about.

I thought I'd put some extra RAM into the *motherboard*, rather than buy a whole new computer.

MOUSE

A small handheld device used to control an arrow on the screen and select an option or space for the arrow by clicking.

Joe loved his new *mouse*—it moved much more smoothly than the old one had.

MULTI-USER DIMENSION (MUD)

A complex role-playing game located online. You go into a set-up environment, play a role, and interact with other people. These may be highly addictive, and many who play them claim to enjoy the world of the MUD more than their own.

You can get to the Black Knight's Realm *MUD* by telnet:sun1.cstore.ucf.edu4000.

MULTIMEDIA

A vague, catch-all term; in general, it refers to things that incorporate more than one type of media—a laser light show with rock music in the background is multimedia.

Her presentation was made more exciting by its *multimedia* approach; Jane used video and audio clips along with the charts and graphs.

MULTIPROGRAMMING

An operating system that allows more than one program to be run simultaneously; it is also referred to as multitasking.

Macintosh and OS/2 are two examples of *multiprogramming* operating systems.

MULTITASKING

(see **multiprogramming**)

MS-DOS

The long name for DOS.

NETIQUETTE

Good manners on the Net, of course.

If you refer to an old post that is no longer up when you post on a newsgroup, that is bad *netiquette*.

NETWORK

A group of computers that are hooked together. If you are part of a network, you can send a file directly from one computer to another.

The Internet is the largest *network* of computers.

NEWBIES

Those who are new to the online world.

"Don't give her a hard time; she's a newbie," said the post after many of the previous entries made fun of Mary's untoward remark.

NEWSGROUP

A discussion group on the Internet revolving around specific topics and consisting of articles or postings made by different users. If you make a contribution, you are posting to the newsgroup. There are literally thousands of newsgroups for any topic imaginable, from support groups for obscure diseases to groups that share erotic stories. You can get a good idea what the group is about from its name.

The Twenty-five Most Popular Newsgroups On The Internet

from *The Internet Complete Reference*, by Harley Hahn and Rick Stout

1. new.announce.newusers
2. misc.forsale
3. misc.jobs.offered
4. alt.sex
5. news.answers
6. alt.sex.stories
7. alt.binaries.pictures.erotica
8. rec.arts.erotica
9. rec.humor.funny
10. alt.sex.bondage
11. alt.activism
12. rec.humor
13. alt.binaries.pictures.misc
14. news.groups
15. news.announce.newgroups
16. soc.culture.indian
17. news.newusers.questions
18. comp.graphics
19. comp.lang.c
20. misc.jobs.misc
21. alt.bbs
22. misc.wanted
23. comp.binaries.ibm.pc
24. alt.sources
25. talk.bizarre

ONLINE

To be hooked, by modem, to a network of computers such as the Internet or a commercial service such as Prodigy.

Marie did an *online* search for that information and accessed the archives at Podunk University.

If you are talking about a piece of equipment, online means being connected properly and ready to go.

We just put fresh paper into the printer, hooked it up and plugged it in; it was *online*.

OPERATING SYSTEM

A program that manages the operations of the computer. The operating system is the interface between the different applications and the hardware.

Some of the different *operating systems* on the market are DOS, PC-DOS, OS/2, and UNIX.

OS/2

An operating system for IBM PCs that has the ability to run more than one program at the same time.

The great advantage of the *OS/2* operating system is that it can have up to twelve programs running at the same time.

PATHNAME

The full name of a file. A pathname will tell you exactly where the file is, from the drive letter to all the directories and subdirectories you'd have to go through to find the file.

She typed in the *pathname* c:\winword\newbook.doc, which told the computer that the file she was looking for was in the C drive, the winword subdirectory under the filename newbook.

PC-DOS

The specific DOS just for IBM: the Personal Computer Disk Operating System.

PERSONAL COMPUTER (PC)

The name IBM gave their microcomputer, and hence, what all those IBM clones have been called. Although the term refers to all microcomputers, it is generally used to refer to IBM clones, as opposed to Macintoshes, or Macs.

The office was purchasing ten more *PCs* for the expansion.

PENTIUM

The name Intel has given to its 586 microprocessor.

The Intel *Pentium* chip is twice as fast as its old 486 microprocessor.

PERIPHERAL

Any hardware that surrounds a microprocessor.

Peripherals in this computer package include a keyboard, monitor, printer, and mouse.

POINT-TO-POINT PROTOCOL (PPP)

Programming that allows a computer to be its own Internet host.

A small company might use *PPP* to establish themselves as a host.

PORT

The spot on the back of a computer into which various peripherals are plugged. There are two main ports: the serial port and the printer port.

After ensuring that the printer was properly plugged into the printer *port*, Alexis attempted to print her document.

POST

Making a contribution to a newsgroup. Your post may be responded to by other posts. Think of a newsgroup as one of those giant community bulletin boards, and your post is the little card you pin up.

Mark *posted* his recipe for guacamole in the recipe newsgroup.

PRODIGY

One of the big three commercial online services (with America Online and CompuServe).

Prodigy is considered to have the best resources for children.

PROGRAM

A set of instructions that tells a computer how to process the information it gets. A programmer is the person who designs the program.

I purchased all the *programming* I need to get my computer running.

PROMPT

Something that appears on the screen that asks the user to perform some task or give some information.

The most recognized *prompt* is the DOS "c" prompt, which looks like this: C>. It tells the user to type in some sort of command right there.

RANDOM ACCESS MEMORY (RAM)

A computer's main memory. It represents how much information a computer can hold and manipulate.

RAM chips may be added to your computer to increase its memory; the more memory a computer has, the more expensive it is.

READ-ONLY MEMORY (ROM)

As the name implies, memory that can only be read, not changed in any way. ROM chips in the computer's hard drive typically contain the instructions that are written when the computer is manufactured. ROM memory stays there, even after the computer is turned off.

The computer's basic input/output system is stored on a *ROM* chip.

RECORDING DENSITY

The number of bits that can be recorded on one inch of the innermost track of a disk. The greater the density, the more information the disk will hold.

We purchased some floppy disks with double the *recording density* for backups.

REMOTE HOST

When making a telnet connection, your computer is called the local host and the one you are connecting to is called the remote host.

The *remote host* he was going to telnet to was only across campus.

RESOLUTION

The number of pixels on the screen. The higher the number, the greater the clarity and sharpness of the image.

As our company runs many graphics applications, a screen with a high *resolution* is very important to us.

RESPONSE TIME

The amount of time it takes for a computer to respond to a command.

The old 286 computers have a much slower *response time* that the new 486s.

SAVE

Transferring information from memory to long-term storage.

Saved information will not be lost if your computer's power source is accidentally turned off.

SCALABILITY

A client-server's inability to handle smoothly the thousands of individual users that a big company may have on its network.

Software writers have been trying to overcome the *scalability* problem in their recent applications.

SCROLLING

Moving the lines displayed on a screen up or down.

We had to *scroll* through three pages of text before we found the line that needed to be edited.

SEARCH

Looking for a file, a bit of information, or a program. Using the right search tool (Gopher, Veronica, Jughead, Archie, for example, on the Internet) will make your search more efficient.

He conducted a *search* for an article on *Jane Eyre*.

SERIAL PORT

A type of port into which you can plug different things, such as a mouse, a modem, a printer, and other assorted peripherals.

The majority of PCs have at least two *serial ports*.

SERIAL LINE INTERNET PROTOCOL (SLIP)

Similar to PPP, only an older version.

SERVERS

PC-like machines that run networks of desktop computers.

By placing two, four, or even eight microprocessors together in a single box, PC manufacturers are able to boost the power of *servers*.

SERVICE PROVIDERS

Companies that give online access; there are commercial service providers and Internet service providers.

Many individuals like to have more than one *service provider*—America Online and CompuServe, for example—so they will have access to more information.

SHAREWARE

Contrary to some people's opinion (and we won't name names), shareware is not free. It's distributed (usually by modem) on the honor system. You can try it out, and if you like the program, the people who wrote it ask that you send them a fee.

With her subscriptions to CompuServe and America Online, Marta had access to thousands of different *shareware* programs that she could download and try out.

SNAIL MAIL

The regular-old-envelope-and-stamp, mail system.

"Please send us your *snail mail* address, in addition to your e-mail address," was written on the top of the petition.

SOFTWARE

The programs that make a computer run; software is needed to make the hardware operate.

The computer system they purchased came with a whole array of *software*, from word processing applications to online services.

SOURCE

The original. Whenever you copy something, the place from which you copy it is referred to as the source.

The computer asked for the *source* drive when I tried to copy that batch of files.

SPOOLING

When information that will be sent to a printer is first sent to disk or to memory to wait patiently until it is ready to be printed.

Spooling increases printer efficiency and reduces the need for extra printers, for if an office sends more than one document to the printer, they will simply line up automatically.

STRING

Any group of characters. If a computer asks for a string of text, it simply means a line of text.

The *string* she entered was eight characters long.

TARGET

When making a copy of something, this is where the duplicate is sent. The final destination is the target.

My *target* for the copy I was making from my hard disk was the "a" drive.

TEXT EDITOR

A special program that edits only text files. It doesn't have any of the fancy-pants formatting of many word processing programs.

She used a *text editor* to type up the ASCII document.

THREADS

In a newsgroup, a series of posts that follow the same topic of conversation.

If you don't want to read any more of a certain *thread*, you can give a "kill" or "junk" command and move on to the next topic in the newsgroup.

TOGGLE

A switch that turns something on, and if pressed it again, turns it off. This applies not only to actual keys or switches but to any program command that turns a function on if you use it, then off if you use it again.

The "caps lock" key on most keyboards is a *toggle* switch.

TUPLE

Another name for a row in a database.

The third *tuple* contained all the information about Joe Bloggs's account.

UNIX

An operating system designed by Bell Laboratories in the 1970s for a multiuser system.

Because of federal regulations in the 1970s, Bell could not market *UNIX* commercially, and so it was licensed to many colleges and universities for their multiuser networks.

UPLINK

In satellite communications, the transmission link between the ground and the satellite.

The crew had some trouble with establishing the *uplink*: the trouble was in the transmission to the satellite from their remote post.

UPLOAD

Sending a file or program from a computer to a network.

Paul *uploaded* his new file management program to the America Online software area so that other users might be able to take advantage of it.

USENET

The "user's network" is a collection of discussion groups called newsgroups. Many Internet sites carry Usenet, one of the most popular features of the Internet.

There are thousands of *Usenet* newsgroups on many different subjects, from politics to movies to jokes.

USER

That's you. Actually anyone who uses a computer is referred to as the user.

"The *user* should then load in the program by typing install," stated the computer manual.

USER-FRIENDLY

A program or computer system that is relatively easy to use for a beginner. Try something that is user-unfriendly and you will know the difference.

The Macintosh icon-based software was said to be very *user-friendly*: you need only click on an icon to bring up a program, rather than remember any commands.

USER ID

The name (pronounced "user eye dee") by which both you and your account are known online. Most people use some variation on their name or a nickname for a userid.

Joe Bloggs used the *user id* JoeB for his Internet account.

UTILITIES

The boring sort of programs in an operating system. They do all that file management stuff like sorting, deleting, copying files, formatting disks, and diskettes and renaming stored files.

A sort *utility* program was used to sort the company's database files by employee number.

VAPORWARE

Software that has not yet been produced.

Micromac's new office-management software looked great on television, but when eager consumers tried to purchase it they found out that it was *vaporware*: the concept had been marketed, but the actual software had not been produced.

VERONICA

A search tool used with Gophers, like its companion, Jughead.

Marie used *Veronica* to search the Gopher sites for file she needed.

VIRUS

A computer program which, like a real-life virus, spreads by duplicating itself into other software. Viruses are malicious—in recent years, virus checks and vaccines have been developed to locate and remove viruses before they do any real damage.

A *virus* can be set to attack at a specified time. The famous Michelangelo *virus* was set to go off on Michelangelo's birthday.

VOICE MAIL

Similar to an answering machine, only a lot more expensive. Callers to a voice mail system are automatically transferred and may leave messages that are digitized and stored on disk for later replay.

The JAN corporation recently installed its new *voice mail* system. You can now call any employee and leave a message on his or her *voice mail* rather than with the secretaries.

WAIS SERVERS

A system used to retrieve information from different databases and libraries in the Internet. You specify which databases you want to search and give a list of keywords to search for; the Wais (pronounced wayz) server will give you a list of articles that you may be interested in.

Wais will display the article you choose after it conducts your search for you.

WORLD WIDE WEB (WWW, W3, OR THE WEB)

One of the most popular services on the Internet, with many multimedia files, WWW allows you to conduct hypertext searches (searches that link you from one source to another).

Ken used his browser to navigate his way through the *World Wide Web*.

WINDOW

A rectangular portion of the screen that contain some sort of information.

Microsoft's Window programs contains neat graphics in *windows* in different program groups, similar to the Macintosh-style *windows*.

WORD PROCESSING SOFTWARE

Software designed for making text documents. Microsoft Word, Word Perfect, and Wordstar are some examples of this type of software.

She wrote her term paper with a Word Perfect *word processing* program.

Chapter 3

MONEY AND FINANCE

> Up and down the City Road
> In and out the Eagle
> That's the way the money goes—
> Pop goes the weasel!

AAA, AA, A RATINGS

Standard & Poor's and Moody's are two of the most famous firms that rate bonds for investors. These ratings refer to the financial stability of the bond issuer. The two rating systems are similar—for example, an AAA from Standard & Poor's is equivalent to Aaa from Moody's.

The city's *AAA* rating from Standard & Poor's made their bonds an attractive investment.

RATING THE BONDS

AAA or Aaa	Best Quality
AA or Aa	High Quality
A	High–Medium Quality
BBB or Baa	Medium Quality
BB or Ba	Moderate, but not well-guarded
B	Risk of future problems
CCC or Caa	Poor quality
CC or Ca	Often in default
C	Lowest rated, poor prospects
D	In default

AMEX

The American Stock Exchange. The American Stock Exchange is the second oldest stock exchange in the United States. Founded in 1842 (originally called the New York Curb Exchange), its rival is the New York Stock Exchange (NYSE).

Wall Street, New York City, is the home to both the *AMEX* and the NYSE.

ANNUAL REPORT

Companies provide annual reports for their investors. They are pretty much what you'd expect—a report on the company's status: what the company did the year before, their ideas and business outlook, a full financial report, including a balance sheet and usually some sort audit done by an outside firm. Because it is designed to make investors feel all warm and cozy about their investments, annual reports are usually big, glossy productions.

The Widget Corporation's *annual report* was quite elaborate, beginning with the full-color photographs of the company plant and president.

ANNUALIZED RETURN

To get an annualized return, you must take a return from a longer period and divide it by the length to get an annual version.

To get the *annualized return* for the JAMS corporation, we took the returns for a five year period and divided by five.

AUTOMATIC TELLER MACHINE (ATM)

You need an *ATM* card, linked to one or more bank accounts to use an *ATM*. These machines allow you to do many of the things you used to stand on line at a bank to do—withdraw money, deposit money, transfer funds from one account to another. Many banks are now part of huge systems (for example NYCE or CIRRUS) that allow you to use ATMs at banks other than your own.

"Thank goodness for the *ATM*!" cried Marcia, as she withdrew money for her cab.

ARBITRAGE

Indexes and futures contracts on indexes may move at slightly different rates. The index futures contract may be for a price a little higher or lower than the actual index. What a trader will do, with a technique known as arbitrage, is buy huge quantities of lower-priced contracts while selling the higher priced ones, and use computer programs to follow these prices. This is a complicated financial maneuver and, as the price changes are so small, it involves trading a great number of contracts to make any real profit.

Arbitragers often affect the market with their purchases, since they often make similar investment decisions.

ASSET-BACKED BOND

A bond that is secured against a specific asset of the company that issues it.

Weehawken Village issued an *asset-backed bond* against the real estate owned by the village.

AT THE MONEY

When an option's strike price for calls and puts is exactly the same, the option is said to be *at the money*.

BACK-END LOAD

A load is a commission charged on a mutual fund. Sometimes there is no initial sales charge—it is assessed when you sell. This is referred to as a back-end load.

Class B mutual funds have a *back-end load*. If only Mary Anne had realized that when she invested—the five percent commission reduced her profit on the sale by $50.

BARTER

Swapping goods or services, rather than using money.

Peter Minuit *bartered* beads and trinkets for the Isle of Manhattan with the Native Americans in 1626.

BEAR

A market characterized by falling prices or an investor who acts with the expectation that prices will fall.

The *bear* market discouraged many investors.

BLUE CHIP

A stock sold at a high price because it is from a large, consistently profitable corporation. There is an unofficial list of blue-chip stocks, which changes from time to time. Large companies like AT&T are generally on the list.

Cicely's father gave her a gift of some *blue-chip* stock when she graduated from business school. He felt it was the foundation of a stable portfolio.

BOOK VALUE

The difference between a companies liabilities and assets. A high book value would mean the company does not have a lot of debt; a low book value would mean that there may be excessive debt.

Jane always made sure to check the *book value* of any company in which she wanted to make an investment.

BOND

A loan made by a group of investors to a corporation or government. The investors earn interest while the corporation or government gets the cash it may need. Corporations and governments may issue bonds to raise money. Investors like bonds because they are relatively safe—there is a fixed maturity date and interest rate set when the bond is issued. Bonds are the most popular investment in the country.

The school district floated a *bond* to finance the construction of a new gymnasium.

How Long Will My Bond Live?
Short Term: Usually a year or less
Intermediate Term: Two to ten years
Long Term: Thirty years or more

BROKER

An agent to buy or sell orders for investments. A full- service broker will give advice on your investments and charge you a higher commission for it. A discount broker will place your buy or sell order without helping you out; they don't charge as high a commission as the full-service broker. A deep-discount broker offers the cheapest service of all, but usually just for investors who trade in large amounts or very frequently.

Since Sal knew exactly what he wanted to buy, he preferred to deal with a discount *broker*.

BULL

A market characterized by rising prices, or an investor who expects the market to rise and invests that way.

It was a *bull* market—prices were moving up steadily.

CALL OPTION

All options are either put or call options. A *call option* is a right to buy.

CAPITAL

Either the net worth of a company or the funds invested in a company by the stockholders and investors.

The Widget Corporation needed to raise more *capital* before they could make the improvements that were so sorely needed for the future.

CAPITAL GAINS

The profit made from selling an investment at a higher price than its purchase price. You need to pay taxes on capital gains; if you purchase a stock for $50 and sell it for $90, $40 is your capital gain, or profit.

Eileen made a $350 *capital gain* when she sold some old stock she'd held onto for years.

CERTIFICATES

In the world of stock market investments, the stock certificate is the actual piece of paper with all the special information about the stock, such as the issuer and the number of shares the certificate represents. A bond certificate is the record of your investment.

Stock *certificates* are often fancy documents.

CLOSED-END FUND

A type of mutual fund. A closed-end fund raises money only once, offers a set number of shares, and trades on the exchange or over the counter.

Closed-end funds are more like regular stocks than their counterpart, open-end funds.

COLLATERALIZED MORTGAGE OBLIGATIONS (CMOS)

A bond backed by a group of mortgages. They are a little more confusing than regular mortgage-backed bonds.

Larry moved to Houston to try his luck selling *CMOs*—they were touted as the hot new investment this year.

COMMISSION

The charge for making an investment. Brokers and brokerage houses charge a commission for buying and/or selling stocks. The commission is generally a percentage of the price of the investment.

David made a $2,000 investment with a broker who charged five percent *commission*. The commission cost him $100.

COMMODITY

An article of trade or commerce, usually an agricultural or mining product.

Sugar, wheat, soybeans, and gasoline are examples of *commodities*.

COMMODITY CURRENCY

Currency made of either gold or silver, or that can be exchanged for gold or silver.

Today, the United States does not have a *commodity currency*; its money cannot be traded for gold or silver.

COMMON STOCK

Stocks in which the investor shares in the success of a company when it does well, or suffers a risk if the company does poorly.

Diane preferred to buy *common stock*; the risks were greater, but she had heard this company was due to make a large profit.

CONSUMER CONFIDENCE

A measure of how typical consumers feel about their current situation and their faith in the future. If people feel good about where they are and where they're going, consumer confidence is said to be high, and the economy will benefit. Even if there is economic recovery, if people don't have confidence in it, they will be hesitant to spend.

Consumer confidence surveys generally check a number of different things: how people feel about their job security, if they would buy big ticket items, or people's willingness to spend on short term purchases.

CONSUMER PRICE INDEX (CPI)

A monthly index from the Bureau of Labor Statistics on what it costs to pay for food, shelter, and other essentials. It is used to adjust Social Security payments and cost of living increases.

Food, clothing, medical care, shelter, entertainment, and even baby-sitting costs are all in the "basket of goods" the Bureau of Labor Statistics uses to calculate the CPI.

CONSCIENCE FUNDS

Also called "green funds," these investments are designed for investors who have a social conscience. They generally shun companies that are not "politically correct," for example, companies that exploit Third World Labor or have bad environmental records.

Marissa and Dal only invested in *conscience funds*—it was part of their campaign to improve the planet.

COUPON RATE

A bond's interest rate.

Bearer bonds used to have coupons attached, which the investor would tear off to redeem. That is why a bond's interest rate is also known as its *coupon rate.*

COVERING THE SHORT POSITION

Selling short is a way to make money in the stock market. In this method, you borrow stocks, sell them, and get the money. Then you hope the price drops. When it does, you buy them back at the lower price, return them, and keep the profit (minus a commission, of course). When you buy them, that is called "covering the short position."

Alice bought 500 shares of World Wide Corp. at $40 to *cover the short position.*

CRASH

A sudden collapse in the value of stocks.

The *crash* of 1929 precipitated the Great Depression of the 1930s.

CREDIT

May pertain to a number of different, but related concepts: it may refer to the reputation a company has for financial strength and integrity.

They were able to get financing on their *credit* rating.

It may also refer to the time a creditor allows for payment of a loan or borrowed amount.

He was extended a two-month *credit* on his account.

Or it may be an accounting entry that a payment has been received.

We will *credit* your account for the amount of $1,000.

CREDIT CARD

A method of purchasing an item and paying for it later. The company issuing the card will usually give a limit to the amount you are able to charge.

James had two *credit cards* with him so that he could charge the items he bought while he was on vacation.

CURRENCY

Simply another word for money. Currency may refer to more than paper or coin money.

On certain islands, shells were used as *currency* to purchase goods and services.

CUSIP NUMBER

The security identification number that is assigned to each stock certificate.

They were able to check the *CUSIP number* to make sure that the stock was legitimate.

CYCLICAL STOCKS

Stocks which go up and down in value according to the state of the economy. Industries that are affected by rises and falls in the economy are most often cyclical.

Airlines typically have *cyclical stocks*: when the economy is floundering, people don't travel as much.

DAY ORDER

If you place an order on the stock market, you may want to limit how much your broker will buy or sell or at what price she will buy or sell. If you want that limit to last for just one day, you tell the broker that it is a *day order*.

The *day order* was canceled automatically at the close of trading, even though it hadn't been filled.

DEALERS

In the stock market, the people who buy and sell stocks for themselves rather than for someone else. They make or lose money based on the difference between the price paid for the stock and the price it sells for.

The *dealers* lost a great deal of money when the price for the commodity dropped substantially and didn't recover.

DEBENTURES

A type of corporate bond. They are issued based on the strength of the issuer's credit, rather than on any specific asset.

The debentures of that institution are very highly rated: they have a solid credit history.

DEBIT

An item of debt, especially one recorded in an account.

The *debit* of $2,000 that Jake owed to his credit company was marked in their accounts.

DEBIT CARD

A debit card is very different from a credit card. A debit account deducts the amount of your purchase from the account set up to service the card. You must have enough money to cover what you buy in the account; no credit is extended to the purchaser.

Because she didn't like to owe money, Lauren got a *debit card* so that the money for her purchase would be taken directly from her checking account.

DEBT COVERAGE RATIO (DCR)

Ratio of net operating income (or NOI) to the annual payments due on debt.

The *DCR* for the company was good—they were not too debt heavy.

DEBT SECURITIES

Investments, like bonds, in which the company or government borrows money from investors to finance something.

The market for *debt securities* has been strong in recent years, as investors have liked the relative security of bonds.

DEEP-DISCOUNT BROKER

A large investor may use a deep-discount broker. These brokers offer greatly reduced commission to those who buy frequently and/or who buy in large amounts.

Because she was buying a large block of stock, Mary Anne was able to use a *deep-discount broker*.

DEEP OUT OF THE MONEY (DOOM)

An option in which the spread between the strike price for puts and the strike price for calls is very large.

DEPRESSION

In a depression, like the one that followed the Stock Market Crash of 1929, the money supply is so tight that businesses slow down and fail, unemployment is high, and the outlook is grim. Because of the situation, there are then checks on the economy to try to prevent the reoccurrence of a full-scale depression.

Unlike the Crash of 1929, the Crash of 1987 did not lead to a *depression*, largely because of regulations and limitations put in place by the government.

DERIVATIVES

An investment is a step or two removed from the actual commodity the investment is about. For example, in a derivative investment, rather than investing in oil, you are betting on the way the oil prices will go. An option is an example of a derivative investment.

Because they are often difficult to grasp, investors frequently lose money when they invest in *derivatives*.

DESIGNATED ORDER TURNAROUND (DOT)

A DOT is a computerized system designed to handle smaller orders of fewer than 1,200 shares on the Stock Exchange.

A majority of trades are handled by the *DOT*, or *designated order turn-around*, system.

DEVALUED

When the value of a currency relative to the value of currency in other countries is lowered. Sometimes a currency is devalued by a country on purpose; other times, the country's economy will cause the currency to be devalued.

Lavaland *devalued* its currency in order to make its exports more attractive on the world market.

DISCOUNT BROKER

A broker who will purchase your shares for you at a lower rate than a full-service broker because he or she does not offer advice.

Because they liked to research their investments themselves, the Greens preferred to use a *discount broker*.

DISCOUNT RATE

The interest the Federal Reserve charges to member banks.

The Federal Reserve Bank is the bank for banks, and it charges a certain rate, known as the *discount rate*, to its member banks that need to borrow money.

DISTRIBUTIONS

The profits a company makes that are dispersed to the investors of its mutual funds.

After the OINK Corp. took out its fees and expenses, the *distributions* we received made the investment quite worthwhile.

DIVIDENDS

The profit that a company pays out to its shareholders.

The board of directors met to decide what the *dividends* would be for that quarter.

DOW JONES INDUSTRIAL AVERAGE (DJIA)

Referred to as "The Dow," this is the most widely referred-to market indicator. It is computed by adding the stock prices of thirty major industrial companies and dividing that number by a factor that adjusts for any distortions.

When a television news show reports that the market has fallen by ten points, it is referring to the *Dow Jones Industrial Average*.

DOWNGRADING

When a rating service drops the rating of a company.

When the company had been *downgraded* from a AAA to A rating, its investors were reticent to reinvest.

DUAL TRADING

When a trader trades both for himself and a client at the same time.

Though *dual trading* is legal, it is not generally considered to be in a client's best interest.

EFFICIENT MARKET

Economists refer to an efficient market as one that is analyzed and has lots of information available about it.

They were confident in their investments, as it was a very *efficient market* they were in—almost all its influential factors were well documented.

ELECTRONIC TRANSFERS

When money is debited and credited from account to account without actually physically passing through anyone's hands.

"I love these electronic transfers!" exclaimed Marcy as she paid for her gas with a debit card, rather than cash.

EQUITY

The value of something, usually a business or a property, after subtracting any outstanding loans or liabilities.

Their house was worth $150,000, but with their $80,000 mortgage against the property, the equity was only $70,000.

EQUITY FUNDS

A type of mutual fund.

EURODOLLARS

U.S. dollars that are on deposit in non-U.S. banks.

Eurodollars may earn interest or be used to make investments in companies (either American or foreign).

EXCHANGE FEES

In the world of mutual funds, a fee charged if an investment is shifted from one fund to another within the same company.

The *exchange fee* was three percent and made her decision to move less attractive.

FAMILY OF FUNDS

The variety of funds offered by a mutual fund company.

The prospectus outlined the *family of funds* offered by that company.

FEDERAL DEPOSIT INSURANCE CORPORATION (FDIC)

The insurance company for banks and depositors. A bank that is FDIC insured will cover your deposits (only up to a certain amount) in case the bank fails or runs into financial difficulty.

The deposits were *FDIC* insured, so Mae didn't run to withdraw her money when she heard rumors about the bank's instability.

FEDERAL RESERVE SYSTEM

The United States' national bank, made of a group of twelve separate banks that regulates, audits, lends to, guards, controls, and administrates to its member banks.

The *Federal Reserve System* plays a huge role in the economy's welfare.

FIAT CURRENCY

Currency that has no value in itself, its value is set by the government.

Fiat currency is the opposite of commodity currency: our current United States dollar is an example of *fiat currency*.

FINANCIAL COMMODITIES

Dollars, pounds sterling, francs, Treasury bonds: all of these things are commodities, just like sugar and pork bellies in the market. They can be traded on the commodities market.

Financial commodities can be exciting investments.

FINANCIAL FUTURES

Futures investments in currency, stocks, and bonds.

The *financial futures* market traders are dealing in commodities that have to do with money rather than wheat.

FIXED-INCOME SECURITIES

An investment that pays a set amount of interest at a set date.

A bond is an example of a *fixed-income security*; that's why so many people like them for investments.

FLOAT

The initial public offering of a bond; if investors go for it, the bond floats.

To raise money for improvements to their building, the SILLY Corp. decided to *float* a bond for $9 million.

FOREIGN EXCHANGE

Changing money from one country's currency to another country's currency

The *foreign exchange* market is not a physical place; it is a network of computers.

Wanna Swap Currencies?

Argentina .... peso	Australia .... dollar	Austria .... schilling
Bahrain .... dinar	Belgium .... franc	Brazil .... real
Britain .... pound	Canada .... dollar	Czech Rep.... .. koruna
Chile................ peso	China .... renminbi	Columbia .... peso
Denmark .... krone	Ecudaor .... sucre	Finland .... markka
France .... franc	Germany .... mark	Greeced .... rachma
Hong Kong ..... dollar	Hungary .... forint	India................ rupee
Indonesia .... rupiah	Ireland .... punt	Israel .... shekel
Italy.................. lira	Japan .... yen	Jordan .... dinar
Kuwait .... dinar	Lebanon .... pound	Malaysia .... ringgit
Malta................ lira	Mexico .... peso	Netherland ..... guilder
New Zealand.. . dollar	Norway .... krone	Pakista .... nrupee
Peru.................. new sol	Philippines.... peso	Poland .... zloty
Portugal........... Escudo	Saudi Arab... iariyal	Singapore .... dollar
Slovak Rep.. ..... koruna	South Africa. round	South Korea. . .won
Spain................ peseta	Sweden .... krona	Switzerland.. . franc
Taiwan............. dollar	Thailand .... baht	Turkey .... lira
United Arab.. ... Dirha	U.S.A. .... dollar	Uruguay .... new peso
Venezuela .... bolivar		

FRONT MONEY

The money needed to get a project going; the money an investor needs before the financing is in place.

They needed $20,000 in *front money* from the various interested investors to investigate the feasibility of such a project.

FULL-SERVICE BROKER

A broker who will not only buy and sell stocks but will give advice. A full-service broker charges a higher commission than a discount broker or deep discount broker, but these two do not offer any investment advice.

We went to a *full-service broker* since we weren't sure what to invest in.

FUND MANAGERS

Since a mutual fund is a collection of different investments—stocks, bonds, etc.—it must be managed. The professional investment company that does this job is called the fund manager.

When they started up their new fund, they first sought the services of a *fund manager* to oversee the project.

FUTURES

Obligations to buy or sell a commodity at a specific day at a specific price. Futures contracts always expire on the third Friday of each month. Because the investor is not investing in an actual commodity, but on how that commodity will perform, futures contracts are derivative investments.

Futures contracts are generally considered risky investments; they can have a big payoff, but can also generate large losses.

FUTURES CONTRACTS

(see **futures**)

FUTURES EXCHANGES

Futures contracts are traded on special futures exchanges.

The United States Futures Exchanges

New York

CMX	The Commodity Exchange
CTN, FINEX	New York Cotton Exchange and its Financial Instrument Exchange
CSCE	Coffee, Sugar, and Cocoa Exchange
NYM	New York Mercantile Exchange
NYFE	New York Futures Exchange

Chicago

CBT	Chicago Board of Trade
CME	Chicago Mercantile Exchange
MCE	Mid America Commodity Exchange

Philadelphia

PBOT	Philadelphia Board of Trade

Kansas City

KC	Kansas City Board of Trade

Minneapolis

MPLS	Minneapolis Grain Exchange

GENERAL OBLIGATIONS BOND

A bond backed by the "full faith and credit" of the issuer. Contrast these with revenue bonds, which may be backed only by the revenue from a specific source.

General obligations bonds are less risky than revenue bonds and usually pay a slightly lower interest rate.

GLOBAL FUNDS

A type of mutual fund that has a portfolio of investments from the U.S. and other countries.

In a *global fund*, the fund manager may move money from country to country depending on where the markets are strongest.

GLOBAL MARKET

The ties among all the markets of the world— when trading stops in one, it begins in another, and the events in one country affect trading in another. The number of international companies as well as electronic worldwide trading also contribute to this global market.

The *global market* explains how markets all over the world affect each other.

GOLD STANDARD

At one time the value of currency was based on the value of metals such as silver and gold. This was called the gold standard.

The *gold standard* disappeared in 1971, when the United States stopped backing its currency with gold.

GOOD 'TIL CANCELED (GTC)

When you make an order on the stock market, you may want to make that a stop order or a limit order (these will limit at what price or how much the broker will buy or sell.) You should tell the broker whether to make your limitations GTC or a day order. GTC will mean that your instructions will stay in place until they are filled, or until you specifically cancel the order.

Since she wanted the stop order to remain in place for a while, Laurice made sure her broker knew that the order was *GTC*.

GREEN FUNDS

(*see* **conscience funds**)

GREENBACK

Slang for dollar.

"I need twenty greenbacks for the bill," Josh joked with Fred.

GROSS NATIONAL PRODUCT (GNP)

The monetary value of all the goods and services, minus depreciation and consumption, produced in a country.

For the third quarter in a row, the *GNP* had increased, indicating that our economy was on the upswing.

GROWTH STOCK

When a stock investment reinvests a profit rather than paying dividends.

When the children were small, their parents invested in *growth stock*; there was no need for the children to receive regular dividends.

HARD CURRENCY

Gold and silver coins, also known as specie.

In the old days, people preferred *hard currency* to flimsy paper currency.

HEDGERS

Investors who protect themselves against changes that may hurt their profit, and their investments are for that purpose.

The makers of cranberry juice *hedged* their investment by buying a future contract on cranberries for a decent price when they heard that there was a drought in the bogs.

HIGH-YIELD FUNDS

Mutual funds that invest in a riskier pool of investments; their potential for profit is greater.

Marcel stayed away from *high-yield funds*; they were too risky for him.

IN THE MONEY

Options where the price comes in above the strike price for calls and below it for puts.

Elaine was so glad that her options were *in the money* for this period.

INCOME DISTRIBUTIONS

One of the ways a mutual fund may pay its investors. This means that they pay from the money earned by the various investments.

Income distributions are paid on different schedules, depending on how a fund is set up.

INCOME STOCK

A stock that pays a regular dividend to its investor.

Maisie preferred *income stocks* so that she would receive a regular payment from her investments.

INDEX FUNDS

Types of mutual funds that attempt to give an investor the same return as she would get investing in all the stocks in a particular stock index.

I invested in a bond market *index fund*—while I myself couldn't invest in every bond on that index, the fund manager did a wonderful job.

INDEX OPTIONS

A right to buy or sell at a set price on a set day on option on an index. It is a bet that a certain market index will rise or fall at a certain time.

Index options are very often too risky for many investors.

INDEXES

A report on the way a market is moving. Investors rely on the myriad indexes to assess how the economy is doing.

The most frequently quoted *index* is the Dow Jones Industrial Average.

INEFFICIENT MARKETS

Markets that are not widely analyzed.

Inefficient markets may be interesting investments for those who are willing to try them.

INFLATION

When money doesn't buy as much as before, due to rising prices.

Prices skyrocketed during the period of *inflation*, as the value of the dollar decreased.

INITIAL MARGIN

The deposit an investor puts down on a futures contract as only a percentage of the cost of the contract.

The *initial margin* on that futures contract was five percent of the value of the contract.

INITIAL PUBLIC OFFERING (IPO)

When a company goes public, the offering of stock for public purchase.

When Cartoonville went public, they made an *initial public offering* of 100,000 shares at $20 each.

INSIDER TRADING

People who work in a company may have specific information about the way that company's stock prices will go. Trading based on that information is insider trading. It may be illegal, and the Securities and Exchange Commission (SEC) monitors that trading very closely.

Because the vice president manipulated the stock price with *insider trading*, he was investigated by the SEC.

INSTITUTIONAL INVESTORS

A company that invests in itself or hold investments in trust for others.

Pension systems are examples of *institutional investors*.

INSTITUTIONAL TRADERS

Traders who trade in large volumes (10,000 shares or more).

Mutual funds are a prime example of *institutional traders*.

INTEREST

The money a borrower pays to a lender for borrowing money. Interest is usually a percentage of the money borrowed. The percentage is called the interest rate.

George was able to finance his purchase at a low *interest rate* of seven percent.

THE RULE OF 72

How long does it take to double your money? If your account has compound interest, you can use this formula:

rate x years = 72

For example, if you have an account at an interest rate of nine percent, your money will double in 8 years.

INTERNATIONAL FUNDS

Mutual funds that invest in foreign markets.
International funds may also be called overseas funds.

INVESTMENT CLUBS

Clubs in which a group of small investors pool their resources to invest in the market.
Membership in our *investment club* is relatively modest—only $50 is needed to join.

INVESTMENT GRADE

Bonds with a rating of Baa or higher by Moody's or a BBB or higher by Standard & Poors.
Mr. Smith advised his children to put their money in *investment grade* bonds only; he felt that junk bonds were silly and risky.

JUNK BONDS

Bonds that are rated Ca or lower by Moody's or CC or lower by Standard & Poors.
Junk bonds may be less expensive, but they are high-risk investments.

LEGAL TENDER

Money that, by law of the government, must be accepted as a payment.
On the United States dollar you will see the words "This note is *legal tender* for all debts, public and private."

LEVERAGE

Remember those levers from physics class? They enabled you to use a small amount of force to produce a larger amount of work. Leverage in financial terms is the same idea: It's when a company uses a small amount of money to make an investment that's worth more. How do they do it? Usually with things like margin calls.
We bought a futures contract worth $10,000 for $1,000 by *leveraging* $9,000 of our investment.

LEVERAGED BUYOUT (LBO)

Using a small percentage of the total money involved to takeover a company. Investors typically make LBOs by borrowing against the assets of the company they are taking over and repaying the loan, from company profits after the takeover is complete.
The sharks at Zippy Corp. performed an *LBO* at Metal Corp. by borrowing huge amounts of money against Metal Corp.'s assets.

LIMIT ORDER

Instructing a stock broker to buy only when the stock falls to a given price. The order may be good until canceled (GTC) or a day order.
We gave the broker a *limit order* to buy the shares when the price dropped to $2.

LIMIT ORDER TO SELL

Just like a regular limit order, only here you're on the selling side. With a limit order you instruct the broker to sell only when the price reaches a certain number.

We gave our broker a *limit order to sell* at $3 per share and not a penny less.

LIQUID

Any asset that can be immediately converted into cash. A checking account is a liquid asset because it can be used in the same basic way as cash. The process of converting assets into cash is called liquidating.

They *liquidated* the estate by selling the properties, so that their parents' assets could be easily split.

LOAD FUNDS

In mutual funds the commission charged to the buyer of the fund. A front-end load fund is one in which the commission is paid up front when the fund is purchased. A back-end load fund is one in which the commission is paid when the fund is sold. A no-load means that there's no commission on the purchase of the fund.

The offer price on that fund was higher than its net asset value, so Fred figured out that it must be a *load fund*.

LOCK LIMIT

A safeguard in the futures market. If a price goes up or down too much, the market will "lock," or stop trading that future until the price stabilizes.

The plummeting price of corn futures set off a *lock limit*.

LONG BOND

The popular name for a thirty-year Treasury bond.

Although it is not really the longest bond around, investors like the stability of the *long bond*.

M1

Liquid assets or "narrow money"; M1 counts only cash and money in checking accounts.

M2

M1 plus savings and small-time deposits, like CDs: anything that can be easily converted into cash. M2 is called "broad money."

M3

M1 plus M2 plus assets and liabilities of financial institutions. This is the most broad definition of the money supply, which includes long-term deposits that may not be easily converted into cash.

MARGIN ACCOUNT

A line of credit with a broker. If you have a margin account, you can leverage, or borrow, up to fifty percent of the price of a stock from your broker. Although interest accrues on the amount, it is not due until the stock is sold, and the profit from the sale goes to the investor, not the broker.

Claudia wanted to invest $10,000 in SPAM Corp. but with her *margin account*, she only had to put up $5,000, and her broker covered the rest.

MARGIN CALL

If the value of a stock that has been bought on margin falls to 75% of its purchase price, your broker will make a margin call: either you put more money into the margin account or sell the stock and take the loss. It's the broker's way of minimizing her risk in your investment.

When the market dropped, the *margin calls* came in fast and furious around the country.

MARKET CYCLES

Up and down shifts in the market, tracked by economists and investors. The market will go up in a bull market and inevitably back down in a bear market.

They mapped out the *market cycles* for the last forty years and concluded that this bear market would turn around soon enough.

MARKET ORDER

An order placed with a broker telling him to buy or sell. You may give a general market order, asking your broker to get a good price, or you may make your order more specific.

We called our broker and placed a *market order* to sell our shares in the Yucco Corporation when we heard of its impending financial problems.

MARKING TO THE MARKET

Futures contracts may move up and down all day long. At the end of each business day on the futures exchange, all the accounts are tallied up by crediting or debiting them. This process is called marking to the market.

When the exchange *marked to the market* at the end of the day, Barney found he had lost $2,000.

MARKUP

The cost added to a bond when it is sold. You can figure out the markup by looking at the difference between current selling price of the bond and the original buying price.

The *markup* on that investment was so high it was hardly worthwhile.

MARRIED PUT

The process of purchasing a stock and a put option on the stock at the same time. If the price of the stock goes down, the value of the put option will increase, because it is an option to sell the stock at a certain price. A married put is a little bit of insurance for some investments.

His loss on the plummeting wheat prices was somewhat offset. He had purchased a *married put* and the value of the wheat options increased.

MEETING THE MARGIN

If the value of your investment drops and your broker makes a margin call (asks you to put more money in the account), you either meet the margin by putting in that extra money to keep your investment, or you must sell your stock.

Johann had faith that the value of his Whiz Toy account would go back up, so he wanted to *meet the margin* rather than sell his stock.

MID-CAPS

Stocks from mid-sized companies; they are smaller than blue chips, but larger than small caps.

Jim called his broker to find out about trading with some *mid-caps*.

MINT

A place where a government manufactures its money. The process of making coins is called minting.

In the United States, coins are *minted* at one of the three government *mints*: Denver, Philadelphia, or San Francisco.

MONETARY AGGREGATES

M1, M2, and M3Â—the monetary aggregates—they are groups of different types of assets.

By tracking the *monetary aggregates*, the Fed sets policy to regulate the money supply in this country.

MONEY

There are many definitions for money, but it is mainly thought of as the commodity that a country officially designates for people to use to purchase goods and services.

We've finally saved enough *money* to put a down payment on that house.

MONEY MARKET FUNDS

A very liquid fund, usually allowing the investor to write checks against it.

We kept a *money market fund* so that we would earn some interest and still have the option to use the money when we needed it.

MONEY SUPPLY

The amount of money a population has to spend at any given time. The money supply naturally includes cash and checking accounts, but it also includes assets that can be sold and turned into cash.

The *money supply* is measured by the monetary aggregates M1, M2, and M3.

MUNICIPAL BONDS (MUNIS)

Bonds issued by municipalities—cities, towns, states, counties—usually for public improvement or operating budgets.

The mutual fund we invested in includes many *municipal bonds* in its portfolio.

MUTUAL FUNDS

A collection of investments managed by a professional investment firm.

There are three main types of *mutual funds*: stock funds, bond funds, and money market funds.

NAKED CALLS

A *naked option call* is the opposite of a covered stock call: In this very risky venture, you are selling an option that will give someone else the ability to buy something you don't yet own. You may have to buy shares of a commodity at the agreed upon price to fill the contract.

We never wrote *naked calls*—they were far too risky for our blood.

NATIONAL ASSOCIATION OF SECURITIES DEALERS (NASD)

A group of brokers linked by an electronic network.

NATIONAL ASSOCIATION OF SECURITIES DEALERS AUTOMATED QUOTATION SYSTEM (NASDAQ)

An automated system that lists almost 5,000 companies' stock prices.

The broker read the *NASDAQ* prices on his screen throughout the day.

NASDAQ MARKET ISSUES

A daily listing of the largest and most actively traded stocks on the NASDAQ.

NATIONAL FUTURES ASSOCIATION (NFA)

A regulating and enforcement agency for the Futures Exchanges.

The *NFA* looked into the trader's practices to assure proper activity.

NEGOTIABLE ORDER OF WITHDRAWAL ACCOUNT (NOW ACCOUNT)

A checking account that bears interest. NOW accounts are usually regulated to restrict how many checks you may write and required minimum balances.

Because they need to keep their funds very liquid but wanted to earn some interest, Zippy Corp. opened a *NOW account*.

NET ASSET VALUE (NAV)

A mutual fund value calculated by adding up the value of all the stocks in a fund and then dividing by the total number of shares; an average price per share.

The Perezes calculated the *NAV* of their funds so that they could figure out what they would be paid if they sold.

NEW YORK STOCK EXCHANGE (NYSE)

The first stock exchange in the country; considered to be the center of market action.

Results of trades conducted on the *NYSE* are published every business day.

NO-LOAD FUNDS

Mutual funds that have no commission charged against them.

Mike always bought *no-load funds*, as it rankled him to pay any sort of commission.

ODD LOT

A stock order that is not a multiple of 100.

The broker charged them extra for the sale, because it was an *odd lot*.

OFFER PRICE

The price it costs you to buy a mutual fund.

The difference between the *offer price* and the net asset value of a fund is the commission charged.

OFFSET

When a trade is neutralized by an opposite transaction. For example, a contract to buy a commodity can be offset by a contract to sell a commodity.

The majority of futures contracts are *offset* by other contracts.

OPEN INTEREST

The number of contracts that have not been offset.

The *open interest* is reported with the other information on futures prices.

OPEN OUTCRY

You've probably seen those movies where traders are all standing around yelling. Orders on the futures exchanges are called out publicly in a cool system where he or she who yells loudest will probably do best.

One of the hardest things for a new trader is the *open outcry*.

OPEN-END FUNDS

A fund that is able to sell shares and grow as people want to buy and join in.

The majority of mutual funds are *open-end funds* and have the ability to grow with their investors.

OPTIONS

The right to buy or sell a commodity for a set price at a set time.

Option's can be great opportunities to take advantage of a price in the future.

OTHER PEOPLE'S MONEY (OPM)

The money borrowed for an investment.

"Don't worry about the deal; it's got OPM financing," the accountant told the company.

OUT OF THE MONEY

When the spread between the actual price of the commodity and the strike price of the option is great.

Out of the money options are risks, but may have a big payoff.

OVER-THE-COUNTER (OTC)

A stock traded without being listed on a stock exchange.

OTC stocks are traded electronically by brokers all around the country.

PAR VALUE

The face value of a bond.

When Smallville issued their municipal bonds, they were initially sold to investors at a *par value* of $2,000 per share.

PAYBACK PERIOD

The amount of time it takes for the money you put into an investment to come back in a return.

The *payback period* for this investment is approximately three years—at that time, you can expect to have earned back the $1,000 you invested.

PAYOUT RATIO

The percentage of its net earnings that a company pays to its investors.

The higher a *payout ratio* is, the more of its earnings a company has to pay out to meet its obligation to its investors.

PENSION FUND

A retirement fund contributed to by both employer and employee, managed and invested by an outside firm.

One of the most impressive benefits at Bradley & Co. was their generous pension fund—employees could contribute up to five percent of their salary and get matching contributions from the company.

PER CENT YIELD

The *per cent yield* of a stock is the percent of the stocks current price that is dividend.

Per cent yield is a way of figuring out a stock's value.

PERSONAL IDENTIFICATION NUMBER (PIN) OR PERSONAL IDENTIFICATION CODE (PIC)

The PIN or the PIC is the special code entered to authorize a transaction with a debit card and functions as a safeguard against other people using your card.

Make sure you don't let anyone know the *PIN* for that debit card, or they may steal from your account.

PRECIOUS METAL FUNDS

A mutual fund in which the funds are invested in mining stocks and gold bullion.

Precious metal funds tend to be very stable and a good solid investment.

PREFERRED STOCK

A stock in which the dividend is guaranteed - it stays the same whether the company prospers or founders.

Petra always bought *preferred stock;* she liked a safe bet.

PREMIUM

When a bond is sold at a price above what you paid for it.

Because her bonds were paying interest well above the market rate, Grace was able to sell them for a *premium.*

PRICE/EARNINGS RATIO (P/E)

The price part is the price of a company's stock; the earnings part is the company's per share earnings in the last year. The price/earnings ratio is just that—the ratio of the price of stock to the company's earnings.

WILY Corp. had a *P/E ratio* of twenty: their price per share was about twenty times the earnings on the stock in the last year.

PROGRAM TRADING

Stock brokers may use an automated computer system for large trades. These program trades may be set to go automatically when a stock hits a certain price.

The Lottsa Brothers Brokerage House relied heavily on *program trading* for their big customers.

PROSPECTUS

A legal document made available to potential investors with financial information about a company.

The *prospectus* for WILY Corp. made Bob worry about its financial security.

PROXY

PROXY STATEMENT

As a stock holder in a company, you have the right to vote on major decisions that company makes—usually one share, one vote. A *proxy statement* is an absentee ballot, so you can cast your vote even if you aren't able to make the annual shareholder's meeting.

Jethro never returned his proxy statement, so no vote of his was counted in the shareholders' vote.

PUBLIC ("GOING PUBLIC")

When a company puts shares in the corporation up for public sale.

After years of private ownership, the expanding WHIZ Toy Corp. decided to *go public* to raise money for future growth.

PUT OPTION

An option to sell a commodity at a set price. The investor in a put option is betting that the cost of the commodity will decrease and, consequently, the option to sell at the higher price will be worth more.

Selling a *put option* is known as writing a put.

RATE OF RETURN

A ratio of income from an investment to the actual investment.

At a *rate of return* of 20 percent, this was an excellent income-producing investment for Whammo.

RATING SERVICES

(see **AAA, AA ratings**)

RECESSION

A moderate, temporary decline in economic activity, usually characterized by things like greater unemployment and decreased consumer spending.

Periods of inflation increase prices, make items unaffordable, and may lead to a *recession.*

REGIONAL EXCHANGES

Smaller versions of the NYSE and AMEX; regional exchanges are located around the country and trade the same stocks as those listed on the NYSE and AMEX.

Results of the five *regional exchanges* are combined with results from the NYSE and AMEX to get a composite trading listing.

REGIONAL FUNDS

A mutual fund that concentrates its investments in one region of the world.

The *regional fund* we invested in was composed of securities from Latin America.

REINVESTMENT FEES

A mutual fund fee (along with management fees, distribution fees, redemption fees, and exchange fees) charged to a fund whenever distributions in the fund are reinvested.

They were able to check the *reinvestment fees* in the fund's prospectus.

REINVESTMENT OPTIONS

Shareholders of a mutual fund with reinvestment options can decide whether to reinvest the money they earn, take it in cash, or perhaps do a little of each.

James checked his *reinvestment options* and decided to put his earnings back into the mutual fund.

RETURN

The profit made from an investment.

He expected a *return* of more than ten percent on his original investment.

REVENUE BONDS

Bonds backed by the revenue, or income, from a specific source. Toll booths, for example, raise the money to pay off Thruway revenue bonds.

Revenue bonds tend to be longer-term bonds. I suppose that explains why those toll booths never close!

REVERSE SPLIT

The opposite of a stock split; a reverse split results in fewer shares in exchange for the number you had. A reverse split may help a stock with an individual share price that is too low.

The Trendy Company did a *reverse split*—two shares originally priced at $3 each were now one share that would be worth $6.

RISK

In the world of finance and investment, the greater the risk, the greater the chance an investment will lose money. High risk investments may be a big gamble, but they lure investors with a possible high return.

Even though the *risk* on that investment was great, the possible return was high enough to make the chance worthwhile.

ROUND LOT

A group of stock shares sold in a multiple of 100.

The *round lot* is usually less expensive to purchase than an odd lot.

SALARY

The compensation received for work.

The term *salary* originally comes from the Latin word for salt, which is how Roman soldiers were paid, as it was so scarce at the time.

SECONDARY MARKET

When bonds are sold through brokers, rather than by the company or issuer directly.

Now available for purchase on the *secondary market*, Thrillville's bonds were a good investment.

SECONDARY OFFERING

If a public company wants to raise even more money, they may issue a secondary offering, which is another chunk of stock.

After Cheapo Electronics issued a *secondary offering*, the price per share of their stock went down.

SECTOR FUNDS

A mutual fund that focuses on a particular sector of industry or the economy.

Precious metal funds are stable *sector funds*.

SECURITIES

Stocks or bonds.

The *securities* were traded by different brokers.

SECURITIES AND EXCHANGE COMMISSION (SEC)

A watchdog agency that regulates the investment industry. The SEC makes sure that investors are properly informed about their investments and that transactions are fair and free from fraud.

The *SEC* investigated a company it suspected of carrying on illegal insider trading.

SELLING SHORT

First you borrow shares from a broker, then you sell them and take the money. You hope the price drops, and then you buy back the same share at a lower price, return the share to your broker, and keep the profit. This funky little transaction is called selling short. Of course it won't work if the price of the shares goes up.

When the price of the shares he'd sold dropped from $10 to $5 per share, Juan was able to buy them back and make a nice profit by *selling short*.

SHARE

Any one of the equal pieces a company's stock is divided into.

He purchased 3,000 *shares* of the best blue-chip stocks around.

SHAREHOLDERS

The investors who buy stock in a company.

The *shareholders* voted on whether or not to have a new stock issue.

SILVER CERTIFICATES

United States dollars printed before 1963 were backed by silver reserves.

Silver certificates are collector's items today, even though they can no longer be traded for silver.

SINGLE-COUNTRY FUNDS

A mutual fund that gets all its investments from a single country.

They always invested in *single-country funds* for small developing countries, with the hope that the new economy would thrive.

SINKING FUND

A cash reserve, is set aside for bond calls when a bond is issued.

They used the *sinking fund* to finance periodic bond calls.

SMALL-CAPS

Stocks from small companies; they may be hard to trade or get information on.

Although the potential revenue from *small-caps* was there, they were too hard to trade for Margaret's taste.

SMART CARDS

Plastic cards used primarily is situations where change is needed—vending machines and the like. The amount is automatically debited from the card each time you use it.

The Mass Transit Authority instituted the use of *smart cards* rather than subway tokens for their new system.

SPECIE

Another word for coins.

The kids loved to collect different *specie* from around the world.

SPECULATOR

One who invests in risky financial transactions just on the promise of making money. Compare the speculator to the hedger, who usually engages in transactions to protect himself.

The number of *speculators* in the market drove the price up.

SPLIT STOCK

If the price of a share of stock gets to be too high, the company may split the stock; there are more shares, but each at a lower price. Often, splitting stocks leads to greater returns for the shareholders.

When the price per share skyrocketed to $100 each, Troll Corp. *split the stock* so that each share was now two shares worth $50 each.

SPOT MARKET

Another name for a cash market, in which things are bought and sold right there, for cash "on the spot."

They always bought commodities on the *spot market.*

SPREAD

In stock markets, the difference between the highest price a buyer asks and the lowest price a seller offers. In the futures market, the spread is the difference between a sell contract and a buy contract on a commodity. When you play around with options, the spread is when you buy and write options for the same commodity at the same time.

In all these cases, the *spread* will dictate how much money an investor makes in a deal.

STOCK

The capital a corporation raises by selling shares. Stock also refers to the certificate that shows ownership of shares. The terms *stock* and *shares* are often used interchangeably.

They bought *stock* in the new Nifty Company when it went public.

STOCK EXCHANGE

A place where stocks and securities are bought and sold.

The Stock Exchanges of the World	
Tokyo	Nikkei 300 index, 225 average, Topix Index
London	FT 30 share, 100 share
Frankfurt	DAX
Zurich	Swiss Market
Paris	CAC 40
Milan	MIBtel Index
Amsterdam	ANP-CBS General
Stockholm	Affarsvarlden
Brussels	Bel-20 Index
Australia	All Ordinaries
Hong Kong	Hang Seng
Singapore	Straits Times
Taiwan	DJ Equity Market
Johannesburg	Johannesburg Gold
Madrid	General Index
Mexico	I.P.C.
Toronto	300 Composite

STOCK MARKETS

(see **Stock Exchange**)

STOCK OPTIONS

(see **options**)

STOCKHOLDERS

The people who hold stock in a company.
The *stockholders* voted down the new stock issue.

STOP-LOSS ORDER

An order telling a broker to sell a stock if it falls to a certain price. It is usually placed by an investor who suspects that the price may drop. A stop-loss order may be good 'til canceled (GTC) or a day order.

When Paul heard that the price of his stock may go down, he called his broker to place a *stop-loss order*, so that his losses would be minimized.

STRADDLE

When an investor makes a straddle trade, he buys an option and writes an option for the same commodity simultaneuosly.

A *straddle* is a way of covering yourself—if the person you've written the option to exercises her option to buy, you can cover yourself by exercising your option to buy with the option you've bought.

STRANGLE

Writing a buy option with a strike price above the market price and a sell option with a strike price below market price.

A *strangle* is another way of providing some insurance for your trade.

STRIKE PRICE

The agreed-upon price you would pay or receive if you exercise your option. If you have an option to buy (call), it is in your best interest if the actual price of the commodity is above your strike price, because you now own an option to buy at the lower price. If you have an option to sell (put), you hope that the commodity's price is lower than the strike price, and consequently your option guarantees you the higher price.

When the wheat prices dropped to $60 per share, Brenda was happy to have an option to buy at a *strike price* of $50.

TAPE

The band of stock quotations that move on a computer screen; the term originated with the use of ticker-tape machines to report stock quotes.

Brokerage firms read the *tape* to get a constant stream of information about stocks.

TAX EXEMPT

Refers to an investment in which the income earned by it (usually in the form of interest) is not taxed. Some investments are city tax exempt, and/or state tax exempt, and/or federal tax exempt.

Municipal bonds, because they are *tax exempt*, are especially appealing to high income people who pay lots and lots of taxes.

TAX-FREE FUND

A mutual fund consisting of investments that are not taxed. *Triple tax-free* means that the fund is exempt from city, state, and federal taxes.

The earnings on the fund were not as high as others, but because it was triple *tax-free*, it was an attractive buy for the resident of that city.

TELERATE MACHINE

The machine that gives the read out of stock quotations, as the old ticker tape used to.

The *Telerate* screen had a constant stream of numbers moving across it.

TOMBSTONE AD

A notice announcing that a security is either being offered for sale or has sold.

Investors check the *tombstone ads* to see what is up for sale, the name of the underwriter, the issue, and the date it will be sold.

TOTAL EXPENSE RATIO

In a mutual fund, the percentage of that fund's assets that are paid as fees.

The *total expense ratio* for Whammy Corp. was low. They had managed to keep down all the fees associated with maintenance on the fund.

TOTAL RETURN

On a mutual fund, the percentage a fund has gained or lost, assuming that distributions are not paid out, but reinvested. Total return may be reported as a year-to-date total return, or as a quarterly, annual, or multi year total return on the fund.

The year-to-date *total return* on our mutual fund was almost ten percent—not bad compared to our other investments.

TRADERS

The people who actually execute the buy and sell orders. Traders must be registered, and they charge a fee for making the trade.

The activity came to a peak as all the *traders* pushed and shoved to get their orders.

TRADING PIT

The area on the floor of an exchange in which the trading takes place. A pit may be divided into areas for different types of trades.

The *trading pit* was a sea of activity; to those who didn't know, it seemed totally out of control.

TREASURY DIRECT

An account established to buy and hold Treasury bonds.

We called our broker and established a *Treasury Direct* account for our Treasury issues.

TRIPLE WHAMMY

You can get a triple whammy when you invest in international stocks because you can make money three ways: the value of the stock may increase, the dividends it pays may increase, and the foreign currency may become more valuable, so it will cost more dollars for someone to buy it.

When the value of the franc against the dollar rose so dramatically, Pete finally realized his dream of getting a *triple whammy* on that investment.

UNDERWRITE

To assume financial responsibility for something.

The venture was *underwritten* by a group of investors.

UNDERWRITER

One who assumes the risk in a new issue of investments by purchasing the issue and reselling it to the public or to a dealer.

Zippy Corp. sold its new stock issue to an *underwriter* who made his profit by reselling to a dealer.

UNDERLYING INVESTMENT

When purchasing an option, the actual thing you are buying.

When the *underlying investment* of foreign currency went up, Alice was glad that she had the call option at the right price.

VALUE STOCKS

Fairly stable stocks considered to have some good growth potential.

James liked to balance out his portfolio with *value stocks* and cyclical stocks.

VENTURE CAPITAL

Money for new businesses. Most investors with venture capital will lend the money but will want to have a hand in running the business.

The savvy investor can take advantage of a fledgling entrepreneur by investing *venture capital* in a new business and lending experience as well as money.

VOLATILE

When a market is *volatile*, prices are constantly changing. The opposite is a stable market, in which prices are more constant.

The Bradleys were wary of investing in such a *volatile* market.

WARRENTS

If you purchase a warrent in the stock market, you are purchasing a right to buy a stock at any time in a certain time period for a set amount of money. If the price of the stock rises above the price you have set, you can buy the stock for a profit. If it doesn't, your warrent will expire and you lose the cost of the warrent.

We purchased 100 *warrents* at $1 each to buy Spamo Corp. stock for $20 a share. When the stock priced soared to $26, we exercised the warrent, bought the stock for the $20, and made a $5 profit on each share, for a total of $500.

WRITING A PUT OR WRITING A CALL

In the land of options, if you sell a put or a call, you are "writing the put" or "writing the call."

Warren was *writing a call* for an investor to buy from him a stock he owned.

YANKEE BONDS

Bonds sold by foreign bond issuers to U.S. investors in dollars rather than their own currency.

Because he was always confused trying to convert foreign currencies to figure out his investments, Dominick preferred *Yankee bonds.*

YIELD

A return on an investment.

After careful planning, Amy was able to yield almost fifteen percent on her original investment of $10,000. She made a profit of $1,500.

ZERO-COUPON BONDS

If you buy a zero coupon bond, interest is built up until the bond matures.

Jack loved to buy *zero coupon bonds* so that he wouldn't be bothered with periodic interest.

ZERO-SUM MARKETS

In a zero-sum market, every gain is offset by a loss.

Futures and options are *zero-sum markets* because every profit someone makes is someone else's loss.

Chapter 4

REAL ESTATE

"Six feet of land was all that he needed."
—Leo Tolstoy

ACCELERATED DEPRECIATION

A tax write-off schedule that allows greater depreciation allowances on an asset in the beginning.

Although he had twenty years to depreciate the asset on his tax form, Mario took an *accelerated depreciation* schedule that allowed him to take a higher depreciation now, when he really needed it.

ADJUSTABLE RATE MORTGAGE (ARM)

A mortgage with an interest rate that may change periodically. The rate is usually adjusted during regular periods (say, every three years) during the life of the loan and is tied to some index or formula.

Because they had heard that interest rates would be falling in the next few years, Donny and Marie felt it would be smart to get an *adjustable rate mortgage*.

ADVERSE POSSESSION

When someone continuously, openly, and spitefully occupies and possesses a piece of real estate with some claim.

AFTER-TAX INCOME

Income after income taxes have been deducted.

Because they were in a lower tax bracket, The Bramleys' *after-tax income* was not very different from their income before taxes were taken out.

AGENT

In the simplest terms, a person who has been given authority to act on someone else's behalf.

Real estate *agents* are given authority by the seller of a home to represent the seller's wishes to any potential buyer.

AGREEMENT OF SALE

A written contract between a buyer and a seller that comes before the actual closing takes place. It lays out all the terms that they have agreed upon for the sale to close.

They signed an *agreement of sale,*which stipulated that the seller would be responsible for the cleanup of the environmental hazards and the buyer would take care of the flood damage.

ALTERNATIVE MORTGAGE INSTRUMENT (AMI)

Any mortgage that is different from a standard fixed-rate, level payment mortgage: for example, gradual payment loan, adjustable rate mortgage, and a reverse annuity mortgage.

AMENITY

A nice thing, a convenience that improves the quality of life.
Amenities on the property included a tennis court, swimming pool, Jacuzzi, and sauna.

AMERICAN INSTITUTE OF REAL ESTATE APPRAISERS (AIREA)

The Appraisal Institute, as it is commonly known, is one of the main professional organizations for real estate appraisers; they confer the MAI and RM designations for appraisers.

The introductory course on real estate appraisal was given by the American Institute of Real Estate Appraisers.

AMERICAN SOCIETY OF REAL ESTATE COUNSELORS (ASREC)

Another professional organization for real estate appraisers; this one gives out the CRE designation.

AMORTIZATION

Paying off a mortgage or any debt with regular, scheduled payments. An amortized mortgage requires regular payments of the loan amount and interest on the loan. The amortization schedule is the schedule of payments that your bank or lending institution may give you.

When Jan and Phil received their *amortization* schedule, it laid out all payments they had to make, broken down to show how much of the payment was principal and how much was interest.

ANNUAL PERCENTAGE RATE (APR)

The amount of the interest paid each year. Even if an advertisement screams out "2% monthly interest!" it must report the *APR* (here, twenty-four percent) as well.

The Truth in Lending act made the bank show the *APR* as well as the periodic interest, but they still used really small print.

ANNUITY

A yearly income.
The will stipulated an *annuity* of $15,000 for the next ten years.

APPRAISAL

An unbiased estimate of a property's value. Most banks require a real estate appraisal before they will give a mortgage on the property. The lender usually refers to the result of this appraisal as "the appraised value."

The *appraisal* put the value of the property at $150,000, even though Ziggy paid $200,000 for it.

PROFESSIONAL DESIGNATIONS FOR REAL ESTATE APPRAISERS

If you are considering purchasing, financing, or insuring real estate, you will probably need the services of a real estate appraiser. Most people are unfamiliar with what type of appraiser is needed. Banks generally maintain an "approved list" of appraisers on file—this means that they will accept an appraisal from someone on that list for the purposes of receiving financing from their institution. Some of the most common terms you might hear in relation to real estate appraisers are:

State Certified: Some states now require that real estate appraisers pass an exam to receive state certification.

MAI: Member, Appraisal Institute. The Appraisal Institute is one of the major professional real estate appraisal organizations. They educate and certify their member appraisers. The MAI designation is one of the highest an appraiser can receive. It indicates that he or she has passed a series of classes and exams and has submitted a demonstration appraisal for approval.

APPRECIATION

Any increase in a property's value.

The property *appreciated* greatly after they put in a fancy pool.

APPURTENANCE

Something that is added to the property and passed along to the buyer with the property itself.

The tool shed was an unsightly but useful *appurtenance*.

ARABLE

Land that is suitable for farming.

After the effects of the drought and toxic waste, that land was no longer considered *arable*.

ARM'S LENGTH TRANSACTION

When both buyer and seller are out on the open market, are not related, and are under no pressure to buy or sell, the subsequent deal they make is an *arm's length transaction*.

Because the sale price was very fair, they had to assume it was an *arm's length transaction*.

ASSESSED VALUATION

The value placed on a house or property for tax purposes. Real estate taxes are a percentage of your assessed valuation, which may bear absolutely no resemblance to appraised value.

An assessor is the person who makes the assessment.

With an annual tax rate of 7% and an *assessed valuation* of $20,000, the property would have $1,400 a year in real estate taxes.

ASSET

Any property with value; may refer to real estate, investments, or personal property.

With the houses, cars, artwork, and investments, the estate had *assets* valued at more than $3 million.

ASSUMABLE MORTGAGE

A mortgage that can be transferred from the seller of the property directly to the buyer. Not all mortgages are assumable.

It made the deal that old Mr. Lapine had an *assumable mortgage*; the buyers were able to take it over at a fixed interest rate that was way below market value.

BACKFILL

Backfill can refer to the process of removing dirt from a construction site excavation, or to the stuff they put below groundlevel around a structure and foundation for support.

They *backfilled* almost 100 yards of soil from the site.

BALLOON MORTGAGE/BALLOON PAYMENT

A loan that has a big final payment, called the *balloon payment*.

The *balloon mortgage* had a monthly payment of $1,000 for five years, with a final balloon payment of $20,000.

BARREN

Lacking any vegetation.

The land had been *barren* for years since the devastating fire.

BASEMENT

The lowest level of a building, either fully or partially below the ground.

They had a finished *basement* with a recreation area for the kids to play in.

BEARING WALL/BEARING PARTITION

A wall or partition that actually supports a part of the building. If a wall is a bearing wall, it cannot be knocked down in a renovation without compromising the safety of the building.

Paul wanted to knock down the wall between the kitchen and the family room, until he found out it was a *bearing wall*.

BEDROOM COMMUNITY

A community outside a major city, from which many of its residents commute to the city to work.

The *bedroom community* of Seascape was only a twenty-minute commute to the city where Mary worked.

BLANKET MORTGAGE

A mortgage for more than one piece of property.

When the contractor built fifty houses on that property, he took out a *blanket mortgage* rather than fifty individual ones.

BINDER

A legal agreement by the buyer of a piece of property to cover the down payment before the final contract is signed.

They signed a *binder* so that the seller wouldn't entertain any more offers on the house.

BLUEPRINT

An architectural plan for construction or renovation of a piece of property. It is called a blueprint because the special paper used is blue.

They needed *blueprints* drawn up for their renovation before they could even think about beginning any of the work.

BONA FIDE SALE

A sale made in which both buyer and seller were acting in good faith, with the intent to buy and sell.

BOUNDED DESCRIPTION

(see **metes and bounds**)

BROKER

A real estate agent, usually licensed, who acts on the seller's behalf to find a buyer for the property. The broker charges the seller a commission if he or she makes the sale.

Although they didn't want to pay a commission, the Jayhawks listed their house with a *broker* because they didn't have time to sell it themselves.

BUILDING CODES

State or local regulations for the design, construction, and use of real estate. May be referred to simply as "code."

Because the inspectors found that the building's electrical system was not up to *code*, they would not grant a certificate of occupancy.

BUILDING PERMIT

An official authorization to build or alter a structure, obtained by submitting a plan to the local or state government.

"You don't even have a *building permit*!" cried the inspector. "You'll have to tear this building down."

BUTTRESS

An exterior wall or building support that gives support by pushing in on it.

The *buttresses* on the church were actually quite beautiful.

BUYDOWN

An additional chunk of money—a percentage of the loan, or points—offered at the closing in exchange for a reduced loan rate.

The Bradley's *bought down* a mortgage to further induce the purchasers of their home—a lower interest rate was a great incentive.

CAP

A limit on charges.

There is a six-point *cap* on the interest rate on the life of that loan: If your initial rate was ten percent, the rate could never be raised above seventeen percent.

CAPITAL
CAPITAL ASSETS
CAPITAL EXPENDITURES
CAPITAL EXPENSES

Money ready for investment. *Capital assets*, in real estate, usually refers to income-producing assets. A *capital expenditure* is an outlay of cash used to buy an asset. A *capital expense* is the money used to pay off the interest and amortization of a loan.

The *capital expenditures* for Jiffy Corporation were high that year; they expanded their company by buying five more buildings.

CAPITALIZATION

A method used by real estate appraisers to convert the income a property produces into a value estimate for that property.

The number used to *capitalize* income is called the *capitalization* rate.

CERTIFICATE OF OCCUPANCY (C OF O)

A certificate issued by the local government that officially allows a building to be occupied. It means that the building has been inspected and that all forms have been filed.

When the Binks sold their business, the buyers realized that there was no *C of O* for the small building in the back—the buyers would not be able to use it until they took care of that.

CERTIFICATE OF TITLE

(see **title**)

CLERESTORY WINDOW

Windows placed at the top of a building for light and ventilation, frequently seen in churches and many modern buildings.

The architect designed the wall to have a row of *clerestory windows* along the top to bring in light without loss of privacy.

CLOSING

A meeting with buyer and seller, as well as any attorneys and bankers involved in the sale of a piece of real estate, at which the final transactions take place. After the closing, the seller takes possession of the property. Not to be confused with the contract signing. Note that *closing* is a noun, but you may use the verb *close* to talk about the meeting.

Approximately two months after Zippy Corp. signed the contract to buy that industrial building, they *closed* on the property.

CLOSING COSTS

There are a number of costs associated with a closing—you don't put all those people in a room for free. The closing costs include things like the transaction fees, the attorney fees, and any other bank and insurance fees. Many banks estimate your closing costs for you when you apply for a mortgage so that you can plan for them.

The *closing costs* were not as excessive as Zippy Corp. had anticipated—they brought plenty of checks with them to cover everything, though.

CLUSTER ZONING

A type of zoning that allows houses to group together with lots of open space around them, as opposed to more normal zoning where the houses are evenly spaced.

The developer of Condo City went to the town to apply for *cluster zoning* in that area.

COLLATERAL

Any asset you offer as a guarantee that you will repay a loan.
Spammo put some of the company assets up as *collateral* for the mortgage.

COMMISSION

A percentage of the price received for the sale of real estate or of the yearly rental of a property, paid to a real estate agent for selling or renting your property.

Even though we made a small profit when we sold that office building, most of it went to the agent's six percent *commission*.

COMMITMENT

A promise by a bank or lending institution that you will get a loan at a specified amount and interest rate. The bank's commitment usually is for a short time.

As soon as they signed the contract on the property, the board at Spammo got a *commitment* from their bank.

COMMON AREA

Any part of a property with more than one tenant that is for use by all the tenants. That area may include parking lots, lobbies, or laundry facilities. The maintenance for that area may be charged to the residents with *common-area charges*.

The office was small, but the building had conference rooms available in the *common area*.

COMMON WALL

A wall shared by two buildings.
In the city, there are many attached buildings with *common walls*.

COMPARABLES (COMPS)

An appraiser gathers a list of *comparable sales* in an area when she does an appraisal on a property. They use these *comparables* to arrive at a value for the subject.

The appraiser was lucky to have five *comps* from sales right on the block of buildings that were almost identical to the subject of the appraisal.

CONDOMINIUM

A special type of residential unit in which the buyer purchases a unit in a residential community. In a condominium, the owner has rights to the inside of his unit and common areas in the community.

The doctors enjoyed the *condominium* they shared: they each took care of their offices and paid fees for the maintenance of a common waiting and reception room and parking area for all their patients.

CONTRACT

In real estate, the buyer and seller sign a contract which commits the two of them to go through with the deal. The actual closing, where they transfer possession of the property, usually takes place a month or two after.

After Whammo agreed to a price for Widget to buy its building, they signed the *contract* and went about getting the financing in place for the closing.

CONVERTIBLE MORTGAGE

A convertible mortgage is one that has the option to change to a different type of mortgage at some point in its term.

Zippy Corp. took advantage of their *convertible mortgage* when they changed their adjustable rate mortgage over to a conventional fixed-rate after five years.

CONVEYANCE

The written record of a real estate transaction; for example, deed, a mortgage, a lease.

The *conveyances* were recorded in the county records; anyone could see how much Whammo paid for Widget's building.

COOPERATIVE APARTMENT (CO-OP)

A real estate transaction in which the buyer gets shares in the corporation that owns the building in return for a special lease on the apartment.

When Alice's apartment building went *co-op*, she jumped at the chance to buy into it at a reduced price.

COUNSELOR OF REAL ESTATE (CRE)

A designation given by the American Society of Real Estate Counselors.

CREDIT REPORT

A report from an independent company of the borrower's credit status—how much outstanding credit and debt the borrower is carrying and how timely payments were.

After the bank received the excellent *credit report* on Zippy Corp., they decided to go through with the loan.

CUSTOM-BUILT HOUSE

A house ordered by a buyer before it is built, with specific amenities added on request; the opposite of a house built on speculation.

The president of Widget insisted on a *custom-built house* so that he could have special cages built in for his exotic birds.

DEBT COVERAGE RATIO (DCR)

The ratio of a company's net operating income (NOI) to its loan payments or debt service.

The Smallville Farmers' and Mechanics' Bank calculated Tweezerman's *debt coverage ratio* to determine whether it would be able to pay back the loan.

DEBT FINANCING

Paying for part or all of a property with borrowed funds.

The Widget Corp's. new building would serve as collateral when they *debt financed* the property with a big mortgage.

DEBT SERVICE

The loan payment, including both interest on the loan and whatever part of the principal.

The *debt service* for Whammy was way too high after they refinanced all their properties.

DEDICATED

Property that is publicly owned and maintained. You usually see this term in relation to roads—the owners may dedicate the road to the town or city so that they are no longer responsible for its maintenance.

The XYZ Development Corp. *dedicated* all the roads in its new development over to Smallville as soon as the homes were completed.

DEED

A written document that conveys any sort of interest in real estate.

Zippy Corp. had a *deed* to that property; they insisted that Widget Corp. stop using it as storage for widgets.

DEED DESCRIPTION

The written description in a deed of all the boundaries of the property.

Because this was such a large and strangely shaped piece of land, the *deed description* was almost a full page long.

DEED RESTRICTION

A restriction on a piece of property that passes through the deed from owner to owner.

When XYZ Developers bid on that property, they didn't know that a *deed restriction* prevented any buyer from dividing the ten acres in any way.

DEFERRED MAINTENANCE

Anything in a property that should be fixed right away. Even though it sounds like it, deferred maintenance does not really mean something that should have been fixed already.

The *deferred maintenance* on the property (primarily the need for a new roof) amounted to almost $20,000.

DENSITY

The number of anything per whatever unit of size. You may have a density that refers to how many people or homes or trees or cars are in a given size of property.

The population *density* in New York City is considerably higher than in Manitoba, Canada.

DEPARTMENT OF HOUSING AND URBAN DEVELOPMENT (HUD)

The department of the U.S. government that handles programs like low-income housing, urban renewal, urban planning, and the like.

This special low-rent public housing was financed partially through a grant from *HUD*.

DEPRECIATION

The loss of real estate value, either by the market or by deterioration of the assets.

The building's *depreciation* was fairly low—it was only two years old and most of the stuff in it was in good physical shape.

DOWNZONING

When the zoning in an area is reduced to fewer buildings in a given area.

After the town had suffered a glut of development, Smallville downzoned the residential area from quarter-acre to two-acre minimum lots.

EASEMENT

Permission to use a portion of someone else's property without owning it. Towns, for example, have *easements* that allow them to install underground lines through private property.

Widget gave Whammo an *easement* that allowed Whammo's employees to walk through Widget's side yard to get to the bus stop.

ECONOMIC LIFE

The amount of time that the buildings on a property add to the value of the property itself.

The *economic life* of that complex may be more than 100 years.

EFFECTIVE AGE

As opposed to the real age, the effective age of a structure has to do with the condition of the building.

Although Spammo's headquarters were almost twenty-five years old, they had replaced so much of the original structure that it had an *effective age* of only five or six years.

EFFECTIVE GROSS INCOME MULTIPLIER

The ratio of the value of a property to the effective gross income that property generates—or the income you'd expect to get minus any losses or vacancies.

ENCROACHMENT

May refer to the act of trespassing on someone else's property, (i.e., "The growth of the apple tree encroached on their neighbor's backyard.") or to an area that gradually changes from one type of use to another.

As the business area in Glenville expanded, it *encroached* on the residential area.

ENERGY EFFICIENCY RATIO (EER)

The ratio of energy output of an appliance to its energy input. Output is expressed in BTUs, and input is expressed in wattage.

They updated the heating and cooling system in the office space to one with a higher *EER*.

EQUITY

The value of an owner's property minus all the outstanding mortgages and liens against that property.

The owner's *equity* decreased when he took out a second mortgage against the property.

ESCROW

An agreement to give money, securities, property, or a similar offering to a third party to hold until it is due to be transferred to the designated person or agency. For example, banks hold money in escrow for their customers real estate tax payments.

The lawyer held the down payment in *escrow* until it was set to go to the sellers of the property.

EVICTION

Kicking someone out of a property.

The landlord finally *evicted* his tenants for non-payment of rent.

EXCLUSIVE AGENCY
EXCLUSIVE RIGHT TO SELL

If you approach a broker to sell a property for you, there are a number of sales agreements you may enter into. An *exclusive agency* listing means that only that agent is given the listing to sell your property. You may, however, sell it on your own and not pay commission to the agency. In an *exclusive right to sell* listing, the agent gets a commission if the property is sold, regardless of who sells it, until the listing expires.

Because Light Bulb City believed that Century 2001 would work harder for them, they signed an *exclusive right to sell* listing for a three-month period.

EXECUTOR

The person given the job of settling the estate of someone who has died; the executor is appointed in the will or by a court. The process of settling the will is called **executing**.

After the *executor* of the estate, Ms. Jamison, had the property sold, she split the money among the remaining six sisters, as the will specified.

FAIR HOUSING LAWS

Federal, state, and local laws that guarantee people of all races and genders freedom from discrimination when buying, renting, selling, or making any real estate transaction.

The landlord was fined for breaking *fair housing laws* when he refused to rent to a group of women.

FALLOW

Land that is not used during a growing season.

The acres and acres of *fallow* land were wasted in this farm community.

FEASIBILITY STUDY

An analysis done by an impartial party as to whether a project would be profitable or useful for an investor.

They hired the consulting firm of Smart & Co. to do a feasibility study for their plan to build a chain of chicken-plucking stores in the region.

FEDERAL HOME LOAN MORTGAGE CORPORATION (FHLMC, OR "FREDDIE MAC")

A federal agency that buys mortgages from lenders, giving them more cash to make new mortgages, and gives aid to the FHA and Veteran's Admistration-backed loans.

The Physical Bank sold a block of their mortgages to *Freddie Mac*.

FEDERAL HOUSING ADMINISTRATION (FHA)

The branch of HUD that insures mortgages and offers low-interest guaranteed mortgages to homeowners.

Urban DevCo. was thrilled to get an *FHA* loan to renovate their offices.

FEDERAL NATIONAL MORTGAGE ASSOCIATION (FNMA, CR FANNIE MAE)

The largest secondary mortgage agency in the country. A secondary mortgage agency purchases mortgages from lenders to help with the distribution of funds. *Fannie Mae* published a standard form for residential real estate appraisals.

Appraiser Co. Inc. was required to fill out a *Fannie Mae* form for any residential appraisals they did for Peach Bank.

FEE SIMPLE ESTATE

An estate that is owned without any outside interests or encumbrances. The fee simple represents all the rights you have in real estate—for example, the right to sell, lease, or use a property.

Most real estate is owned as a *fee simple estate*.

FIRST MORTGAGE

The mortgage that takes precedence over any other mortgages or liens against a property.

When Urban DevCo. sold its property, the owner of the *first mortgage*, Peach Bank, was paid before any of the other lenders.

FLOATING RATE

A variable rate that moves according to some other rate (usually the prime rate).

The *floating rate* Tweezerman received on the line of credit was always three points above the prime rate.

FREE AND CLEAR

Describes a property with no mortgages or liens outstanding.

After making the final payment of their thirty-year mortgage, the Manns proclaimed, "We finally own a house that's free and clear!"

FUNCTIONAL UTILITY

How well a building serves its purpose; when assessing functional utility, an analyst takes into account what the market wants and how the building is designed and laid out.

The small rooms, bad traffic flow, out-of-date architectural design, and poor layout all made the *functional utility* of that building very low.

GENERAL CONTRACTOR (GC)

The person or company that supervises the building or renovation of a structure.

The GC on the project was responsible for hiring the subcontractors: the plumber, electrician, carpenters, and sheetrockers, for example.

GENERAL PARTNERSHIP

A partnership in which each partner is completely responsible for any liabilities.

Henrietta was hesitant to enter into a *general partnership* with her ex-husband for their business venture, Divorces Corp.; he was so unreliable.

GENTRIFICATION

The process of renovation that takes place as an upper- and middle-class clientele begin buying into low-income neighborhoods and upgrading them, so that the people who lived there before gentrification are often priced out of their own neighborhoods.

In the 1980s, yuppies *gentrified* many derelict neighborhoods in Bigville by buying buildings cheaply, fixing them up, and raising property values substantially.

GIRDER

A horizontal beam that is a main support in a building.

As the construction on the new office building in downtown progressed, you could see construction workers walking along the *girders* to inspect the steel frame.

GOVERNMENT NATIONAL MORTGAGE ASSOCIATION (GNMA, OR GINNY MAE)

A federal corporation under HUD that purchases FHA-insured mortgages on the secondary market and issues mortgage-backed securities that are federally insured.

GRADE

A general term that refers to the level or slope of a property. "Street grade" means at the level of the street. A "10 percent upgrade" means the property slopes up 10 percent from the horizon line. "Grading" a piece of land means giving it the slope and look necessary for proper drainage and appearance.

After the bulldozers *graded* the property, they were ready to put in the roads.

GRADUATED PAYMENT ADJUSTABLE MORTGAGE LOAN

A mortgage in which payments gradually increase over a set period and the interest rate is adjusted from time to time according to some index.

Because they were just starting out, MelonWorks thought a *graduated payment adjustable mortgage* would be a good idea; their payments would increase as their business took off, and they were confident that interest rates would be going down as well.

GRAZING CAPACITY

The maximum number of whatever type animal that can graze in an area without doing permanent damage.

The farmer looked at the numbers for *grazing capacity* before purchasing his cattle at the auction.

GROSS BUILDING AREA

Total floor area, including basement and garage area, but not including unenclosed areas, such as decks.

The *gross building area* of that property came in at 10,000 square feet.

GROSS INCOME

The total income from a business or property.

Their *gross income* that year doubled from $1 million to $2 million when they opened a whole new chain of stores.

GROSS INCOME MULTIPLIER (GIM)

The ratio of the value of a property, and the gross income the property generates. The GIM is used to estimate the value of the property.

The market in Snakeville supported a GIM of five, so when Harvey heard that Snakeville Oil Center was for sale for $5 million he knew that it had better generate at least $1 million a year in business.

GUARANTEED MORTGAGE

A mortgage that has some second party backing up the borrower in case he or she cannot pay.

Because of his poor credit rating, Harry was only able to get a mortgage if he told Peach Bank that he would get a *guaranteed mortgage*.

HOUSING STARTS

Newly constructed housing units; also used as an economic indicator—one of the ways the government has of evaluating the strength of its economy.

Housing starts were up for the third consecutive quarter this year, indicating that we are pulling out of the recession.

HOUSING STOCK

The total number of housing units.

The *housing stock* in our area was inadequate for the influx of people that Papco was bringing in for its new factory.

INDEXING

A method of changing the rate on an adjustable rate loan according to some set index—the Federal Reserve's Prime Rate, for example. A loan that is indexed may be called an *indexed mortgage*.

The bank was *indexing* all the current loans to its best customers to three points above the prime rate.

INDEX LEASE

A lease that allows rent to move up or down, according to some set index.

The Musico Corp. preferred an *index lease* in which their rent was set according to the cost of living index.

INSTITUTE OF REAL ESTATE MANAGEMENT (IREM)

A professional organization for real estate managers, which gives CPM and AMO designations.

INSTRUMENT

A legal document.

The mortgage *instrument* had clearly outlined all the conditions for indexing the mortgage.

INTEREST

Money paid to the lender by the borrower for making the loan.

The *interest* paid on that loan was almost as high as the principal.

INTEREST-ONLY LOAN

A special loan in which the borrower pays back the interest for a set time and then the principal in one lump sum at the end of the loan period.

Because their starting resources were scarce, Zippy Corp. took out an *interest-only loan* for capital expenditures.

INTERIM FINANCING

A temporary loan that is usually paid off as soon as the full financing for a project comes through.

To get the project going, ABC Co. was able to get some *interim financing*.

INTERNAL RATE OF RETURN

The annual yield or rate of return on an investment for the term of ownership.

The appraisers, accountants and bankers all calculated the *internal rate of return* for the ten-year period that Zippy Corp. intended to own the factory before deciding if it was a good investment.

JOINT TENANCY

The legal term that applies to ownership by more than one person where the rights are transferred to the survivor(s) if one party dies.

As husband and wife, they had *joint tenancy* in the building.

JOINT VENTURE

A limited legal agreement between partners temporarily paired for a specific business venture

Strawberry Co. and Rhubarb Co. entered into a *joint venture* to produce pies for the youth market.

KICKER

An incentive or bonus for an investment. A kicker may be required by a lender to increase their potential return on the loan they're making.

Peachy Bank took a chance with Zippy Corp.'s new venture, so in return they asked for a 10 percent *kicker* on the loan. If Zippy made the million-dollar profit they claimed, they would owe Peachy Bank an additional $100,000 bonus.

KNOCK DOWN

Construction material that arrives unassembled but totally ready to be assembled and installed.

To save a little money, Ted ordered *knock-down* jambs for all the doors in the house.

LALLY COLUMN

A steel support column.

There weren't enough *lally columns* in the building's basement to meet the building code in that area.

LAND CONTRACT

An installment plan. In this specific type of contract, the buyer pays the seller in installments and uses the land, but doesn't receive deed or title until the sale price has been paid.

ABC Corp. decided to sell its property using a *land contract* rather than give Acme Corp. a mortgage; that way they could hold the deed and foreclose easily if Acme didn't perform.

LAND PLANNER

A consultant who studies an area and gives reports on things like traffic, amenities, appropriate use of natural and manmade resources, quality of life, etc. Land planners typically work for municipalities to develop a master plan for a community.

Mr. Brown, *land planner* for the town board of Smallville, realized that the plan for an industrial park on the waterfront was not an appropriate use—the canal leading to it was virtually impassable.

LANDSCAPING

As a verb, *landscaping* means the adding of trees and shrubs and ornamental plantings to a site.

As it was so dry in their area, the company *landscaped* with cacti and rock gardens.

As a noun, *landscaping* refers to the actual plantings.

The *landscaping*, with its dead, scraggly shrubs, was so horrid that it made the property unsaleable.

LATE CHARGE

A penalty a borrower must pay for not making a payment on time.

Because their mortgage payment was due by the tenth of each month and they never paid until the twelfth, Whizzy accrued hundreds of dollars in *late charges*.

LAYOUT

The arrangement of the rooms themselves in a building, and the space and details in each room.

The *layout* of that house, designed by the famous Igoguchi Design Team, was so simple and useful that the house sold immediately.

LEASE

The written, legal document for a rental agreement.

The terms of the *lease* specified that the lessee was liable for any damage to the property.

LESSEE/LESSOR

In legal talk, the tenant/the landlord.

LEASED FEE ESTATE

If you own property and lease out some or all of it, your ownership interest is called "leased fee," meaning that you are entitled to collect rents and other potential income from the property, and have the right to repossess the property when the lease ends.

When Jim hired the appraisers to value his property, they were able to value his *leased fee* interest, since he rented out the space to several retail stores.

LEASEHOLD ESTATE

The ownership interest that the person or company renting a property has. The leasehold estate includes the rights to use and occupy the property, but not the right to sell.

Mr. Brown realized that his leasehold was valuable when he sublet the factory he'd rented from ABC Corp. for $1,000 a month to XYZ Corp. for $2,000 a month.

LEGAL DESCRIPTION

The section, block, and lot numbers of a property that identifies it on a tax map, or a metes and bounds description in a deed or legal document, that identifies the boundaries of the property.

When Robert went to the county records to investigate the Hammer Headquarters building, he had the section, block, and lot numbers for the property, as that was how all the legal description was filed.

LIEN

Any interest in a property used as collateral for a loan.

Their mortgage was the primary *lien* against the Whammo's headquarters.

LIFE ESTATE

The use of a property and all the rights associated with it for one's lifetime.

When the Bumsteads let their son buy their house, they retained a *life estate* so that they could continue to live in it until they died.

LIQUIDATION PRICE

A price below market value, usually when there is not enough time to let the property stay on the market and get the best price. The price the seller ends up taking is called the liquidation value of the property.

When Zippy Corp. went bankrupt, it had to sell off many of its real estate holdings at a *liquidation price.*

LOAD-BEARING WALL

(see **bearing wall**)

LOAN-TO-VALUE RATIO

Ratio of the amount of money a bank will lend for a mortgage to the value of the property that is being mortgaged; there may be a maximum percentage according to state law.

Because the bank needed a *loan-to-value ratio* of less than 80 percent, the Smothers Company could not take out a mortgage of more than $800,000 on their property appraised at $1,000,000.

LOFT

Attic space, or the upper floor of a warehouse or factory.

In the 1980s, many artists rented inexpensive *loft* space in the warehouses in downtown New York City, because they liked the open floor plans.

MANAGEMENT FEE

The fee, usually monthly, paid to the management service of a building.

The co-op charges included a monthly *management fee*, sent to the co-op management company.

MARKET STUDY/MARKETABILITY STUDY/MARKET ANALYSIS

A market study or analysis will give an independent analysis of a market in a specific area, including economic resources, levels of unemployment, current and historical market trends in the area, etc. The marketability study will analyze more specifically how well a particular project may be sold or leased in that area.

The XYZ Corp. ordered a *marketability analysis* before they started their 500-unit residential development—they wanted to see what the chances were of selling all the units within two years.

MARKET VALUE

Market value is defined as the most probable price a property will sell for in a competitive market with an informed buyer and seller who are not under any duress during the sale.

The real estate appraisal, assuming all fair market conditions, gave the *market value* for the subject property as of October 4, 1989.

MEMBER, APPRAISAL INSTITUTE (MAI)

A professional designation given by the American Institute of Real Estate Appraisers.

The bank would only accept an appraisal report that had been reviewed and signed by an *MAI*.

METES AND BOUNDS DESCRIPTION

A type of legal description that gives the boundaries of a property as defined by different landmarks on the property.

The Metes and Bounds Description of the Zippy Industrial Complex

Beginning at a point 100 feet south of Main Street, running thence south 81 degrees, 3 minutes 0 seconds west, 700 feet thence north 90 degrees, 60 minutes, 5 seconds east, 1000 feet thence north 81 degrees 3 minutes, 0 seconds east, 720 feet thence south 85 degrees, 60 minutes, 5 seconds west, 950 feet to the point of beginning.

MIXED-USE ZONING

Zoning which allows different types of buildings to go into the same area , such as a mix of residential, office, and commercial space in one district.

The developer wanted to take advantage of the *mixed-use zoning* by building up a whole section of downtown with residential apartments, convenience stores, and office space.

MORATORIUM

Putting a stop to something for a specific time for a specific reason.

The town of Smallville placed a two- year *moratorium* on commercial building to assess the environmental impact on the water supply.

MORTGAGE

A legal document for a loan in which property is held as collateral for the loan.

Before they could close on their new office complex, Razors "R" Us had to obtain a *mortgage* in the amount of almost a million dollars.

MORTGAGE BROKER

A person who will match a buyer to a mortgage lender, usually for a fee as some percentage of the desired loan amount.

Ames Construction Corp. hired a *mortgage broker* to find them the best financing available for their new development.

MORTGAGE TERM

A loan's term of repayment.

Sminkley Consulting preferred a *mortgage term* of only five years, rather than a longer fifteen, twenty or even thirty year term.

MULTIPLE LISTING SERVICE (MLS)

A computerized service of real estate sales listings, distributed among sales agents so that more than one office will work on the sale of the property.

Jan thought it would be best to list with a broker who had *MLS*, so that her home would be shown by as many agents as possible.

NATIONAL ASSOCIATION OF REALTORS (NAR)

The main trade and professional organization for the real estate industry; includes such professional organizations as the American Institute of Real Estate Appraisers (AIREA), American Society of Real Estate Counselors, Institute of Real Estate Management, and Realtors National Marketing Institute," among many others.

NATIONAL REGISTER OF HISTORIC PLACES

A listing of historic sites that are considered worthy of preservation. Homes and buildings that are registered must be maintained according to strict guidelines.

Once the headquarters of Spiffo had been put in the *National Register of Historic Places*, they had to have approval for any renovation to the structure and facade of the building.

NET INCOME MULTIPLIER

Similar to gross income multiplier, but instead utilizing the net income rather than the gross income.

NET INCOME RATIO

The ratio of the net operating income to the effective gross income multiplier.

The bank calculated the *net income ratio* for Zippy Corp. to estimate how well they were managing their property.

NET OPERATING INCOME (NOI)

A busines's income after deducting its operating expenses, from its gross income but before deducting any debt service.

After deducting all the monthly overhead and salaries, Limey Corp. had a yearly *net operating income* of about $1 million, as compared to a gross income of almost $2 million.

NONBEARING WALL

A wall that is not important to a building's integrity.

When the architect made plans to tear down walls on the first floor to open the rooms into one large space, she made sure they were *nonbearing walls*.

NONCONFORMING

A building or part of a building that no longer conforms to zoning ordinances, as the zoning came into effect after the structure was built. Nonconforming structures are legal because when they were built they were conforming. Also called "legally nonconforming."

That extension is a *nonconforming* use because by the new zoning ordinance there must be a minimum of twenty feet between it and the property line.

NUISANCE

Something that takes away from the enjoyment of a property.

That garbage dump emits such a toxic odor, it is a public *nuisance*.

OCCUPANCY RATE

The income actually received from a rental property as compared to what would be received if the property was 100 percent rented out.

Because of the recession downtown, our main office building has an *occupancy rate* of only about 50 percent.

OFFER

A price and any special terms that a potential buyer makes to a seller.

They ABC Corporation made an *offer* of $1 million for the purchase of the XYZ Building.

OFFSITE IMPROVEMENTS

The sidewalks, curbs, water and sewer mains, streets, lights, and other anemnities that service a property.

The developer was responsible for the *offsite improvements* in her new housing project.

OPEN-END MORTGAGE

A mortgage in which the principal may be increased, like a line of credit, up to a specified ratio of asset value to debt.

Tweezerman maintained an *open-end mortgage* with Peachy Bank, as they knew they would need additional money in the next few years.

OPERATING EXPENSE RATIO

The ratio of a company's operating expenses to its effective gross income.

The right to buy, sell, or even lease a property within a certain time frame and under certain terms.

PERFORMANCE BOND

A bond usually given by a developer to the local municipality to guarantee that all improvements will be completed.

Smallville always required hefty *performance bonds* to insure that local developers would fix all roads and install proper utilities before they were finished with their jobs.

POINT

One point represents 1 percent of a mortgage amount and is usually charged by the lender to cover the costs of getting the mortgage. If you are applying for a mortgage of $100,000, for example, and there are Three points in fees, you will have to pay an additional $3,000.

To provide an incentive for borrowers, American-European Bank was offering a mortgage with no *points*.

POTENTIAL GROSS INCOME MULTIPLIER (PGIM)

Ratio of value of a property and how much income that property could potentially generate.

PREFABRICATED HOUSE (PREFAB)

A house that is constructed in pieces in a factory somewhere and then put together on a site.

They couldn't believe how quickly the *prefab* was assembled after all the pieces had been delivered.

PREPAYMENT PENALTY

Okay, you want to pay off a mortgage before it is due. You'd think they'd be happy. Read your contract—some mortgages have a prepayment penalty, which simply means if you pay it off early, you may have to pay some sort of fee, usually a small percentage of the loan amount.

XYZ Corp. had thought about paying off the balance of the loan, but the *prepayment penalty* made it wiser to wait and pay it off on schedule.

PRINCIPAL

The amount of money borrowed as distinguished from the interest, which is accrued on the principal.

In the first few years of mortgage payments, you are paying almost all interest; very little of the *principal* is paid back.

PROPRIETARY LEASE

The lease a co-op corporation gives to a co-op apartment owner to allow for payments to cover the operating costs and debt on the complex.

When Debbie bought a co-op apartment to live in, she signed a *proprietary lease* with the co-op board to pay the monthly expenses.

PROSPECTUS

A legal document that sets forth the terms of an offering for sale.

Before they purchased the condominium, the owners of Zippy Corp. gave the *prospectus* to their lawyers for review.

QUITCLAIM DEED

A deed that passes any rights or interest in a property to another person.

Typically, *quitclaim deeds* are used when parties are unsure if they have rights to transfer, or the title to a property is so screwy that it can't be transferred with a guarantee.

As all the town records had been lost in the great flood of 1926, the purchasers of the Bumstead estate got all the possible heirs to sign *quitclaim deeds* so that they could get free title.

REASSESSMENT

A process of giving a property, or a whole group of properties a new assessed value.

The county was going to *reassess* all the homes this year to placate homeowners who claimed that newer homes were assessed at a much higher level than were the older homes.

RENT

Money paid for the use of real estate or other property.

Bradley and Co. could *rent* out office space in its building for up to $20 per square foot.

RESIDENTIAL PROPERTY

Property used for homes, as opposed to commercial or office space. Single-family homes, apartment buildings, and co-ops all fall in this category.

Teenyville was almost all zoned as *residential property:* they didn't want much commercial use in their small village.

REVERSE ANNUITY MORTGAGE (RAM)

A mortgage specifically designed for older homeowners who have little if any outstanding debt on their homes. In this mortgage, you are essentially borrowing against the value of your home and receiving a monthly payment from the bank. At some point, often upon the death of the mortgage holder, the note is due. The longer the note is held, the more money is due to the bank.

To supplement her income, Sophie took out a *reverse annuity mortgage*—she received a monthly check from the bank, and they would deduct the amount from the sale of her house after she died.

RIGHT-OF-WAY

A right to cross over someone else's property for some reason.

The B&O Railroad had a *right-of-way* through the rear of that industrial property for its train tracks.

ROLLOVER MORTGAGE

A mortgage in which every few years (or whatever time specified), the mortgage amount is technically due yet the lender typically carries over the amount to a new mortgage with a new interest rate. May also be called a *renewable mortgage*.

Zippy Corp. liked to have a *rollover mortgage* so it could take advantage of better interest rates every few years.

SECONDARY MORTGAGE MARKET

Banks often sell their mortgages to government and private agencies in order to have more cash on hand to extend new mortgages.

The ABC Company found out that its loan with Peachy Bank had been sold on the *secondary mortgage market* to Ginnie Mae.

SEED MONEY

Money needed to start a real estate venture—usually for land, legal advice, and market study.

The BIG Development Corp. estimated it would need close to $200,000 in *seed money* to purchase the property, obtain all the permits, and study the market.

SPECULATION BUILDING (SPEC)

A builder either builds a custom building specially ordered by a client, or builds on spec, meaning that he doesn't have a buyer when he builds.

That whole development was built on *spec* and yet the houses were so nicely designed that they sold immediately.

STRIP DEVELOPMENT

A commercial area that is built up with a strip of stores along the road, as opposed to single stores or a large mall.

Along Route 9, you can see the enormous amount of *strip development*—tons of little strips of shops that you can pull right up to.

TAX ABATEMENT

An official reduction or complete suspension of real estate taxes after the initial assessment has been made on a property.

The J52 City *tax abatement* allowed the investors to pay little real estate tax on the property while they renovated it.

TAX ROLL

The list of people or companies who pay property tax in a given municipality.

After Quick Corp. purchased that office building, its name was entered on the *tax roll* for Smallville.

TAX SALE

The sale of property to pay property taxes.

The taxes on that office building in downtown were so delinquent that it finally went up for *tax sale*.

TENANT

Someone who either owns a property or more often leases a property.

TITLE

Proof of ownership. In real estate, title is exchanged at the closing. The title must be clear of all outstanding liens before it is passed on.

XYZ Corp. bought *title* insurance to protect themselves against any claims against their property rights.

TRACT

A piece of land, usually a large parcel that may be sub-divided.

BPL Construction was looking for an attractive *tract* of land for his new ten-home development.

UNIMPROVED LAND

Land that is vacant, with neither buildings nor the necessities required for buildings, such as roads and utilities.

The price for *unimproved land* is much less than for that parcel that already has the roads and utilities in place.

UTILITIES

Public services, such as water, gas, electricity, and telephone.

The cost of *utilities* in our county is much more than in neighboring counties.

VACANCY RATE

Ratio of vacant space in a building to total space. May also refer to the ratio of total rents for the vacant space to the total rents for the building.

Alice Corp. has had a terrible time renting out office space in its new downtown building—it has an almost 100 percent *vacancy rate*.

VALUATION

The estimating of value. A real estate appraisal report may also be called a *valuation* report.

Bradley and Co. did a *valuation* of the insurable assets of that company for its insurance forms.

VARIABLE RATE MORTGAGE (VRM)

A mortgage in which the interest rate will change according to some set index.

We found out that our mortgage's interest rate decreased by almost two full points when our *variable rate mortgage* was readjusted after two years.

VARIANCE

(see **zoning variance**)

WRAPAROUND MORTGAGE

A mortgage that is added to and includes an old mortgage. In a wraparound mortgage, the new lender will assume the obligation to pay off the old mortgage.

When the Banklees' sold their home, they issued a *wraparound mortgage* to the Jones'—it would encompass their old loan plus the additional amount the Jones' needed.

Chapter 5

TAXES

"Our new Constitution is now established, and has an appearance
that promises permanancy; but in this world nothing can be
said to be certain, except death and taxes."

—Ben Franklin

ABATEMENT

An exemption from paying penalties on late taxes.

Because their building burned down in that tax year, BradCo. received
an *abatement* of the penalties they normally would have had to pay for late
filing of income taxes.

ABOVE THE LINE

The deductions made on gross income to get your adjusted gross income.

Above the line deductions, which include things like IRAs, are taken before
standard deductions.

ADJUSTED GROSS INCOME

Total income minus any legitimate tax adjustments.

Jay had an annual salary of $50,000, but his alimony payments reduced
his *adjusted gross income* to about $20,000.

ADJUSTMENTS

Similar to regular deductions, these are applied to gross income.

Some of the *adjustments* to gross income allowed by the IRS are IRA
or retirement plan contributions, alimony payments, and part of your self-
employment tax.

ALLOWANCES

An exemption from some part of the tax that is automatically withheld
from your paycheck. The fewer allowances, the smaller the paycheck.
Allowances can be calculated on the back of a W-4 form.

Because Paul had three children and owned his own home, he took the maximum number of *allowances* on his W-4 form.

ALTERNATIVE MINIMUM TAX (AMT)

A tax designed to stop those with lots of income from paying too little tax. At a certain level, you must calculate both income tax and, with another form, the *alternative minimum tax*. Then—you guessed it—you get to pay whichever is more.

Only a small percentage of the population paid the *alternative minimum tax*, the government's assurance that no one who makes a lot of money pays too little in income tax.

AMENDED RETURN

A form filed to correct a mistake on a tax form.

Because the accountants miscalculated the charitable deductions for Whammo, the company had to file an *amended return*.

AUDIT

The most dreaded word in the language of taxes: the Internal Revenue Service audits or examines a number of tax returns each year. This whole process is designed to check all the numbers you have reported to ensure the income tax payment is correct. Several things might trigger an audit: unusually high deductions, unusually low income, unusual entries, etc. Some taxpayers are chosen for auditing completely at random.

Because they had itemized an unusually high number of business deductions that year, Zippy Corp. was *audited* by the IRS.

BRACKET

(see **tax bracket**)

BRACKET CREEP

In a period of inflation, salaries will rise, but with them prices. Prior to 1985, you would have had to take another hit from inflation—increased taxes with your higher salary. Since this wasn't really fair, to avoid this phenomenon, known as bracket creep, income taxes are indexed to inflation.

In the 1970s, due to bracket creep, the employees of Zippy Corp. were not happy to get their pay raises—they just meant more taxes.

BREAKS

(see **tax breaks**)

CAFETERIA PLANS

(see **salary reduction plans**)

CAPITAL GAINS

Profit made from selling an investment at a higher cost than the purchase price. Taxes must be paid on capital gains: If you purchase a stock for $50 and sell it for $90, $40 is your capital gain, or profit.

When Tweezerman sold its factory at a profit of $200,000, it had to pay *capital gains* on that amount.

CAPITAL LOSSES

Money lost on the sale of an investment or property.

Jack's accountant broke the bad news: The *capital loss* he took on the sale of his Porsche was not a tax deduction.

CHARITABLE DONATION

Money donated to a charity or nonprofit organization; these gifts are tax-deductible.

The money that XYZ Corp. donated to the local civic organization qualified as a *charitable donation* and gave them a sizable deduction on their corporate tax.

COLLECTION

If an account is sent to collection, that means that it is overdue enough that a company is willing to send it out to a private company to collect. Since these companies take a percentage of what they collect, most businesses will first attempt to collect the account themselves.

The account executive at Zippy Corp. informed Smothers that if his boss didn't pay the bill soon, Zippy would have no choice but to send it to *collection*.

CORPORATE INCOME TAX

A tax on the profits made by a corporation.

The president of Zippy Corp. was dismayed at how much *corporate income tax* his company had to pay after such a profitable year.

CUSTOMS DUTIES

Taxes on imports; also called "tariffs."

When that country raised its *customs duties*, they discouraged much of the import business.

DEDUCTIONS

Expenses subtracted from the amount of taxable income. Medical expenses that are not reimbursed by insurance are deductible.

After all his *deductions* had been added together, James had effectively brought his taxable income down to only $20,000 from his salary of nearly $30,000.

DEFERRED COMPENSATION

Salary or bonuses that are not paid during the year in which they are earned, but later, usually after retirement.

The CEO of Whammo Corp. decided to take this year's bonus as *deferred compensation* so that he would not have to pay taxes on it until after he retired.

DEPENDENTS

Relatives or full-time household members who depend on you for support. For most people, dependents are either children or elderly parents.

Because John's mother received more than half of her support from him, he was able to claim her as a *dependent*.

DEPRECIATION

A method of computing the loss of value of an asset. Depreciation of certain assets can be taken as income tax deductions.

Even though Yippy lost several hundred thousand dollars on its new building, the *depreciation* allowance made it a boon at tax time.

DISCRIMINATE FUNCTION SYSTEM (DIF)

A computer program that looks through tax returns and scans for possible errors or fraudulent entries—one way the IRS pulls returns for audit.

The *DIF* pulled out the corporate tax return from Zippy Corp. for review—luckily the human check on it afterward gave it a clean bill of health, and Zippy Corp. was not audited.

DISPOSABLE INCOME

The income remaining after taxes.

David's *disposable income* was very low that year, because he didn't have many exemptions or deductions and ended up paying a lot of income taxes.

EARNINGS

Income you get the old fashioned way—you earn it. Contrast earned income to investment income, such as interest.

Marge's *earnings* were up this year—thank goodness, because her interest from investments had dropped to practically nothing.

EFFECTIVE TAX RATE

The percentage of total income that is actually paid in taxes. This usually differs from the marginal tax rate because each chunk of income is taxed at a different rate.

Margie's Effective Tax Rate vs. Margie's Marginal Tax Rate

Margie had a banner year with her new sales route—she earned $97,000. Here's how she was taxed:

The first $38,000 of her income is taxed at 15 percent.	$ 5,700
From $38,001 to $91,850, she's taxed at 28 percent.	$15,078
That last little bit from $91,851 to $97,000 is taxed at 31 percent.	$ 1,596
This is Margie's Total Income Tax.	$22,374

Divide it by Margie's Total Income $97,000.

Her *effective tax rate* is 23 percent.

Her *marginal rate* is the rate she pays on the last dollar; 31 percent.

ESTATE TAXES

If someone dies leaving an estate of greater than $600,000, the government imposes an estate tax.

The lawyer told them how lucky they were than Great Aunt Vanessa's estate was not much more than $550,000—they would escape the *estate tax*.

ESTIMATED TAX

This is not a problem if you have a regular job and don't generally have to do things like estimate your salary. But if you're one of those people who is self-employed, you have to make periodic tax payments yourself, and to do that you have to estimate how much tax you will owe.

Assuming she would have a year about as successful as last year, Amy made quarterly *estimated tax* payments based on her earnings from last year.

EXCISE TAX

A tax on certain consumer items, such as alcohol, tobacco, gas, guns, and airline tickets. These taxes are collected by government departments and used for special purposes, such as highway repair.

The price on cigarettes has risen greatly due to an increase in the *excise tax* on tobacco.

EXEMPTIONS

An exemption is a condition allowing the payment of less taxes; for example, being married or having children. The difference between an exemption and a deduction is that a deduction refers to an expense.

When Mike filled out his W-4 form, he marked four *exemptions*, one for being married and three for his children; his withholding tax was severely reduced.

FEDERAL INSURANCE CONTRIBUTIONS ACT (FICA)

The act which requires an employer to contribute half of an employee's Social Security and Medicare taxes. These taxes are called *FICA* taxes.

Jeremy paid $15,000 in *FICA* taxes, and his employer contributed another $15,000.

FILING STATUS

Whether a taypayer is filing as married or single.

Jeremy marked his W-4 form's *filing status* as married, filing a joint return so that he would pay taxes at the lower married rate.

How Can I File? A List of Filing Status Possibilities

Single
Head of household
Married, filing a joint return
Married, filing separate returns

FLAT TAX

A tax in which everybody pays the same percentage.

Jerry Brown, with his proposal of a *flat* 12-percent income *tax* on all citizens, didn't win much popular support.

GENERAL ACCOUNTING OFFICE (GAO)

The government office that monitors the IRS and other federal financial expenditures.

The *GAO*, established in 1921, oversees financial transactions and reports to the public.

GIFT TAX

A tax required on a monetary gift or gifts, but only after a specified amount in the space of a year.

When Marty received another $5,000 from his mother that year, he knew he'd have to pay *gift taxes* on the money she kept giving him.

GROSS INCOME

To the IRS, gross income is gross taxable income: salary, any investment earnings, and any other income subject to income tax.

Because the gift from his mother was under the amount subject to gift tax, Arnold did not include it in his *gross income*.

HEAD OF HOUSEHOLD

A person who maintains a home for at least one dependent but is not married.

Jeanne filed as *head of household*—she had two children living with her—so that she could take advantage of a lower tax rate, even though she was single.

INCOME SHIFTING

Moving reported income into another year or to another person (for example, as a gift to a child), or arranging investments so that taxes are paid on certain income in a year in which income would probably be lower.

By receiving the last payment on his book this January rather than last December, Mark used *income shifting* to even out the tax burden—he didn't expect to make much money this year.

INCOME TAX

A tax imposed on personal or business income.

In the United States, *income tax* is progressive—the more you make, the higher the percentage of your income is taken out for taxes.

INHERITANCE TAX

A state tax imposed on the heirs of an estate. An estate tax is based on the whole estate before it is divided, and the inheritance tax is on the individuals who receive the money. Not all states have an inheritance tax.

Barkley had to pay an additional *inheritance tax* on Uncle Binkley's generous bequest.

THE INTERNAL REVENUE CODE

The tax laws in the United States.

The IRS is responsible for administering taxes according to the *Internal Revenue Code*.

THE INTERNAL REVENUE SERVICE (IRS)

A branch of the United States Treasury Department that collects income tax and enforces the tax code. It can impose penalties, seize property, or take whatever it feels is necessary to collect taxes.

Petra called the *IRS* to get a set of tax forms and instructions sent to her.

INVESTMENT INCOME

Income received from various investments and taxed as a salary.

The additional *investment income* Linda had from the stock split that year put her into a higher tax bracket.

JEOPARDY ASSESSMENT

A procedure in which the IRS may seize property immediately if it thinks the property is about to be hidden to escape taxation.

To prevent the president of Slimy Corp. from hiding those properties, the IRS moved quickly and used *jeopardy assessment* to seize them.

JOINT RETURNS

If you are married, you and your spouse have the option of filing separate returns or a joint return. The tax liability is usually different, so couples need to figure out which is best for them.

Mary and Joe decided to file a *joint return*; they paid less income tax on their combined salaries than they would have had they each filed separately.

KEOGH PLAN

(see **retirement plans**)

LOCAL TAXES

Taxes collected through local municipalities, in addition to state and federal taxes.

After paying the federal, state, and *local taxes*, the profit Zippy Corp. made on its investment was relatively modest.

LUMP-SUM DISTRIBUTION (OR PAYMENT)

Receiving a total agreed-on payment at once, rather than in smaller payments.

When Mr. Banko received a *lump-sum payment* at his retirement, he had to pay quite a substantial income tax on the amount.

LUXURY TAX

An excise tax on an expensive item. Luxury cars, very expensive jewelry, and large boats are examples of items that may incur a luxury tax.

They decided to get the smaller BMW—it was slightly less expensive and would not have a *luxury tax* imposed on it.

MARGINAL TAX RATE

The rate paid on the last dollar of income earned—the highest tax rate paid.

Even though Margie paid an effective tax rate of 23 percent, her *marginal tax rate* was the rate charged on the last few thousand dollars of income— 31 percent.

MARITAL DEDUCTION

A deduction exempting a spouse from estate tax when an estate is passed from one spouse to the other spouse upon his or her death.

Thanks to the *marital deduction*, Marion didn't have to pay any estate tax on what she inherited from her husband.

MARRIAGE PENALTY

A facet of the old tax code by which many married couples paid more together than they would have as two single people. This problem was minimized by the 1981 Tax Act, though some high-income married couples are still penalized.

The *marriage penalty* made it impossible for Biff and Boo Binkley to get a break on their income taxes—they paid more now than when they were single.

NET WORTH

The value of all assets, minus any debts.

After adding up his real estate—worth over $500,000—and subtracting the mortgages (only $100,000), Michael realized that his *net worth* was well over $400,000.

NOTICE OF TAX DUE AND DEMAND FOR PAYMENT

Notice the capital letters? This is serious. This is the official notice that the IRS sends if you haven't paid up in full, and there's no more discussion on the subject. This is the beginning of a collection.

After Evan had been audited and was found to owe an additional $2,000, he received a *Notice of Tax Due and Demand for Payment*.

OFFICE OF MANAGEMENT AND BUDGET (OMB)

A presidential advisory office that helps develop the federal budget.

The *OMB* sent a proposal to the president regarding the new federal budget.

PASSIVE INCOME
PASSIVE LOSSES

Sources of income (or losses) resulting from any businesses in which one is not an active participant.

Abby noted on her tax forms the *passive income* generated from the rental of her investment property in Alabama.

PENSION PLANS

(see **retirement plans**)

PERSONAL EDGE TAX

(see **tax software**)

PROGRESSIVE TAX

Paying higher taxes in proportion to higher income. The income tax in this country is progressive—the higher your income, the greater the percentage of it you must pay.

Most people favor a *progressive* income *tax*—they believe it is fairer if the people with the most money pay the majority of the taxes.

PROPERTY TAX

A tax on the value of real estate. In some states, cars and other personal property are subject to property tax as well.

The *property taxes* in our county were so high they made it nearly impossible for all but the very rich to purchase a home.

REAL ESTATE TAX

(see **property tax**)

RECAPTURE

A tax regulation allowing the government to tax some of an asset either depreciated over serveral years or paid out early.

When David sold his house, even though its value was depreciated, he was forced to *recapture* some of the value and pay taxes on it.

REFUND

A tax amount returned after overpayment.

Fred was thrilled to discover that not only did he not owe any taxes, but that he would be receiving a *refund* of $500.

REGRESSIVE TAX

Any tax in which everyone is taxed at the same rate. The reason? The lower an income, the higher the percentage paid out to a regressive tax.

When David, who makes $100,000 a year, pays 10 percent tax on a $1,000 purchase ($100), he is paying out only 0.1% of his income to the tax. If Paul, who makes only $20,000, buys the same item and pays the same $100 in tax, he is paying 0.5% of his income for that tax—that's because it is a *regressive tax*.

RENTAL INCOME

Income received from the rental of real estate; it is taxable income.

The *rental income* from their upstairs apartment brought Masie and Phil another $2,000 a year in taxable income.

RETIREMENT PLANS

The government allows an employee and his or her company to put away a certain amount of income to be used after retirement. This income is exempt from taxes until used. If the money is used before retirement, it is subject to taxes and penalties. Because of their tax advantages—and the impending doom of the Social Security system—retirement plans are very popular.

How Shall I Retire? A User's Guide To Retirement Plans

Company Plans

These include pension funds and profit-sharing plans. Company retirement plans are typically funded almost completely by your company. You may be allowed to add to it, but typically you must use your taxable income.

401(k) Plans

This is another special type of company plan. In it, you are able to contribute to the plan (up to a certain amount) and not pay any income tax. Often, companies will match part of your contribution.

403(b) Plans

Similar to the 401(k), but for teachers and employees of nonprofit institutions.

Individual Retirement Accounts (IRA)

An account you set up yourself. Most people who are covered under a company plan cannot deduct the contribution they make to an IRA from their income. If you have no company retirement plan, IRA contributions of up to $2,000 per person are deductible from your income.

Simplified Employee Pensions (SEP)

For small company employers who have no formal company plan, the SEP allows them to set up IRA-like accounts for their employees. SEPs are simpler than pension plans, because they are not as strictly regulated.

Keogh Plans

A retirement plan (pronounced KEY oh) for the self-employed and employees of a small, unincorporated business. Maximum contribution is figured as a percentage of your income. You usually need to hire a professional planner to set up the Keogh plan.

RETROACTIVE TAXES

Any taxes paid on income during a certain time frame falling prior to the enactment of a tax law.

When the new tax code was passed this August, it *retroactively* raised the rates for income received any time back to January.

SALARY REDUCTION PLANS

Employee options that allow an employer to take money out of a paycheck for things like retirement plans, insurance, and day care. The money taken out reduces your taxable income. These are sometimes called cafeteria plans, as employees can pick and choose those options they wish to pay for.

Dominick's company offered voluntary *salary reduction plans*, such as employee contributions to retirement plans, that enabled him to pay less in taxes.

SALES TAX

A state tax on certain purchases; a percentage of the total purchase of taxable items.

Bob bought a new suit for $500, but with the 5 percent *sales tax*, the bill came to $525.

SIMPLIFIED EMPLOYEE PENSIONS (SEP)

(see **retirement plans**)

"SIN TAX"

An expression for a tax on cigarettes or alcohol.

Raising the *"sin tax"* had two benefits: increased revenue and also an increased incentive for people to quit.

SOCIAL SECURITY TAX

A tax withheld from a paycheck to finance the Social Security system (primarily for retirees and disabled people). Social Security, with the Medicare tax, is part of the FICA tax withheld from a paycheck.

Mike had $5,000 dollars withheld from his paycheck last year in FICA, part of which was *Social Security tax*.

SURTAX

A tax added to another tax.

The proposed luxury tax was a new *surtax*—it would add an additional 10 percent tax on an item on which you already paid regular sales tax.

TAX BRACKETS

The different income levels that qualify an individual or company for different tax rates. Because we have a progressive income tax, there are different tax brackets.

The LaMattas fell into the highest *tax bracket*, 39.6 percent, as their taxable income was more than $250,000.

TAX BREAK

Anything that allows one to pay less in taxes. Deductions and exemptions are examples of tax breaks.

Congress enacted a new tax code, which, with its lower overall rates, gave a *tax break* to all the population.

TAX COMPLIANCE MEASUREMENT PROGRAM (TCMP)

The random selection by the IRS of taxpayer returns to audit.

The Smiths, chosen for audit through the *TCMP*, had to provide the IRS with complete proof of all their deductions.

TAX COURT

(see **United States Tax Court**)

TAX EVASION

The act of purposely not paying a tax you know you should pay.

The IRS brought Slimy Corp. up on charges of *tax evasion*, for purposely not reporting the income they received from Box Co. the year before.

TAX GAP

The general term used to describe the difference between the actual amount paid in taxes and what should have been paid. The difference is usually because of errors or intentional evasion of taxes.

The *tax gap* is probably not as high as some people think, as most individuals and businesses in this country comply pretty well with tax law.

TAX SHELTER

A legal way to exempt part of income from taxation.

Because the income Jay put into his IRA was exempt from income tax, it was a great *tax shelter*.

TAX SOFTWARE

Specialized software that helps individuals and businesses fill out their federal and state tax returns; some programs help with tax planning as well.

Some Popular Commercial Tax Software Packages

Turbo Tax

Personal Tax Preparer

TaxCut

TAXABLE INCOME

Income subject to tax: for example, earned income, interest and dividends from investments, rental income, gambling winnings, and alimony income. Inheritance income is an example of income that is usually tax-free.

After Edna added up all her *taxable income*, which included her rental income and the income from her investments, she had to pay taxes on almost $100,000.

TAXPAYER IDENTIFICATION NUMBER (TIN)

A Social Security number.

The form asked for the *Taxpayer Identification Number*, so Joey filled in his Social Security number.

TRANSFER TAX

Estate and gift tax; this category refers to a tax paid on assets that go from one pocket to another.

Between the estate taxes they paid on Grandma's estate and the gift tax they paid on the money Aunt Mary gave them, the Smith's paid most of their taxes in *transfer taxes*.

UNEARNED INCOME

Income from sources other than salary, wages, tips, etc.

John added the income from his investments and rentals and realized that his *unearned income* was much higher than he had originally anticipated.

UNITED STATES TAX COURT

The place where IRS claims can be contested.

When he lost the audit, John took the IRS to the *United States Tax Court* to plead his case.

VALUE ADDED TAX (VAT)

A national sales tax added to retail items. It is very popular in Europe, where some countries charge a VAT of nearly 20 percent.

Marie couldn't believe how much higher the prices were in Britain than in the United States until she remembered that they included a *VAT*, which she could have refunded later.

WITHHOLDING

A portion of income taken out of a paycheck for various taxes or employee plans. Withholding is used for income taxes, Social Security taxes, pension plans, and the like.

When Marty filled out a new W-4, he added the extra exemption for his dependent children, to reduce the amount of *withholding* and increase his weekly take-home pay.

Chapter 6

INSURANCE

"What a man has, so much he's sure of."
—Miguel de Cervantes

CHECK OUT THE FINANCIAL HEALTH OF YOUR INSURANCE COMPANY

Best Insurance Reports rate health and life insurance companies. The highest rating, an A++, was only given to a little over 10 percent of all companies rated last year. You can find Best Insurance Reports in your library, or call BestLine at 900-420-0400 ($2.50 per minute).

ACTUARY

The person who calculates all those charts of risks and costs for insurance, called actuarial tables.

Actuarial tables produced by *actuaries* show life expectancies for different age groups and desirable weights for different ages and heights.

ADJUSTER

The insurance company employee who settles the amount the company will pay for a claim.

The *adjuster* was on the site immediately after the fire to calculate the damages and offer an initial payment until the full settlement was made.

ANNUITY

A special type of insurance that provides a yearly income for the holder of the policy.

Because his company did not have a retirement plan, Jack bought an *annuity* from his life insurance company to pay out when he retired.

CASUALTY INSURANCE
CASUALTY LOSS

Casualty insurance covering a general, unexpected loss, called a casualty loss, due to an accident, fire, catastrophe, or company negligence. These things are called casualty losses.

That *casualty insurance* saved ABC Corp. after the huge fire wiped out their plant.

CLAIM

A request made by an insured party for payment from the insurance company.

After the terrible explosion, Acme Corp. made *claims* in excess of $1 million.

COMPREHENSIVE INSURANCE

Insurance covering all types of possible problems: comprehensive medical insurance combines a basic insurance and major medical insurance; comprehensive business insurance would cover any liabilities that were not specifically included.

Acme Corp. was glad to have a *comprehensive* liability *insurance* policy when Mr. Binky brought suit against them for his carpal-tunnel syndrome.

COPAYMENT

The amount of money paid directly to the doctor or care provider when services are received; the balance is paid by the insurer.

Since Jan had a *copayment* of only fifteen dollars, she wrote a check to her doctor for that amount and the rest was billed to her HMO.

DEDUCTIBLE

The amount an individual is liable to pay; any amount above the deductible is paid for by the insurer.

When the damage to the car amounted to $1,052, Eileen decided that it wasn't worth it to make a claim since she had a *deductible* of $1,000.

DISABILITY INSURANCE

Insurance that covers salary in case a disability prevents an individual from working.

The company offered *disability insurance*, so Jane was covered after the accident kept her out of work for almost a year.

GRACE PERIOD

A time frame (often a due date) in which a payment can be made without penalty.

Their insurance policy gave XYZ Corp. a thirty-day *grace period*, so they weren't too worried that they had to pay the bill a week after its due date.

HEALTH MAINTENANCE ORGANIZATION (HMO)

A group health insurance policy that typically emphasizes preventative medical care by covering routine doctors' visits as well as payments due to sickness. HMOs use a list of participating physicians and hospitals that must be used for coverage.

When our company joined the *HMO*, we were given a list of approved doctors and asked to choose a primary care physician.

INDEMNITY

Protection or insurance against loss.

The company had *indemnity* against the fire due to its casualty insurance.

INSURER

The insurance company.

As *insurer*, State House Insurance Corp. reviewed all the claims made for loss.

LIABILITY INSURANCE

Protection against any claims made if someone is injured or property is damaged on your premises.

When their neighbor slipped and broke her arm on their front step, the Browns were glad to have *liability insurance* to cover her claim against them.

LIFE INSURANCE

(see **whole life** and **term life insurance**)

FIRST-TO-DIE AND SECOND-TO-DIE POLICIES

There are two special kind of life insurance policies that couples may carry:

The first-to-die policy covers both spouses but only pays out at the time of the first spouse's death, with the idea that a family may need coverage for the remaining members.

The second-to-die policy is just the opposite—both spouses are covered, but no benefit is paid until the second spouse dies. The idea here is that, for some couples, there's plenty in an estate for the remaining spouse, who can receive the estate without tax, but the family, who must pay inheritance tax, would need coverage.

PREMIUM

The charge for insurance. Premiums are usually paid annually, semi-annually, or quarterly.

The annual *premium* for Mary's term life insurance rose this year from $100 to $120.

PRIMARY CARE PHYSICIAN

In an HMO, the primary doctor you must see before seeing any specialist. The primary care physician makes a referral to a specialist physician.

Since Dr. Bones was my children's regular pediatrician, we named him as their *primary care physician*.

TERM LIFE INSURANCE

Life insurance that lasts for a specific term—if the insured person lives, the policy expires and he receives nothing. If he dies in that term, the beneficiary receives the death benefit. Term life insurance is less expensive than whole life insurance. Typically, the annual premium rises as the insured gets older.

Because Jack was only worried about having insurance until his kids were grown, he got a *term life* policy that would expire when he was sixty, and the last of his children was twenty-one.

UMBRELLA

A policy giving an extra liability insurance with regular insurance.

The Smiths had a $2 million *umbrella policy* in case they were sued for any damages that occurred on their property.

WHOLE LIFE INSURANCE

A life insurance policy that accrues value; it will last the lifetime of the insured unless it is canceled, in which case there is a cash surrender rate. The annual premium is usually set and does not rise, although it is more expensive than term life insurance.

Because Jake always wanted to be sure to leave something for his family, he invested in *whole life insurance*.

Chapter 7
ACRONYMS AND ABBREVIATIONS

ABA American Bankers Association

ADP automated data processing

AI Artificial Intelligence

AMA American Management Association

AFL-CIO American Federation of Labor—Congress of Industrial Organizations (AFL-CIO)

AMEX American Stock Exchange

AMI alternative mortgage instrument

AML adjustable mortgage loan

AOL America Online

APB Accounting Principles Board

AIREA American Institute of Real Estate Appraisers

AMT alternate minimum tax

APR annual percentage rate

ARM adjustable rate mortgage

ASCII American standard code for information interchange

ASREC American Society of Real Estate Counselors

ATM automated teller machine

BBB Better Business Bureau

BBS bulletin board system

BIOS basic input/output system

BPS bits per second

BOL bill of lading

CD certificate of deposit

CD-ROM compact disc, read-only memory

CEO chief executive officer

CFP certified financial planner

CFO chief financial officer

CFC chartered financial consultant

CFTC Commodities Futures Trading Commission

CMO collateralized mortgage obligation

C OF O certificate of occupancy

COO chief operating officer

CIF cost, insurance, freight

CMO collateralized mortgage obligation

COD cash on delivery

COLA cost of living adjustment

CPA certified public accountant

CPI Consumer Price Index

CPU central processing unit

CRE Counselor of Real Estate

CUSIP Committee on Uniform Securities Identification Procedures

D & B Dun & Bradstreet

DBA doing business as

DCR debt coverage ratio

DIF discriminate function system

DJIA Dow Jones Industrial Average

DOOM deep out of the money

DOS disk operating system

DOT designated order turnaround

EEC European Economic Community

EEOC Equal Employment Opportunity Commission

EER energy efficiency ratio

EFT electronic funds transfer

EGA enhanced graphic adaptor

EPA Environmental Protection Agency

FAA Federal Aviation Administration

FAS free alongside ship

FASB Financial Accounting Standards Board

FAQ frequently asked questions

FAX facsimile transmission

FCC Federal Communication Commission

FDA Food and Drug Administration

FDIC Federal Deposit Insurance Corporation

FHA Federal Housing Administration

FHLMC, FREDDIE MAC Federal Home Loan Mortgage Corporation

FICA Federal Insurance Contributions Act

FIFO first in, first out

FNMA, FANNIE MAE Federal National Mortgage Association

FOB free on board

FTC Federal Trade Commission

FYI for your information

GAAP generally accepted accounting principles

GAO General Accounting Office

GATT General Agreement on Tariffs and Trade

GC general contractor

GIGO garbage in, garbage out

GIF graphic image format

GIM gross income multiplier

GNMA, GINNIE MAE Government National Mortgage Association

GNP Gross National Product

GPM graduated payment mortgage

GPO Government Printing Office

GRM gross rent multiplier

GTC good till canceled

HMO health maintenance organization

HUD Housing and Urban Development

IBM International Business Machines

ICC Interstate Commerce Commission

IMF International Monetary Fund

I/O input-output

IPO initial public offering

IRA Individual Retirement Account

IRC Internet Relay Chat

IRR internal rate of return

IRS Internal Revenue Service

K OR KB kilobyte

LAN local area network

LBO leveraged buyout

LCD liquid crystal display

LIFO last in, first out

LTC less than carload

LTV loan to value ratio

MAI Member, Appraisal Institute

MB OR MEGS megabyte

MBA master of business administration

MGIC Mortgage Guarantee Insurance Company

MHZ megahertz

MICR magnetic ink character recognition

MLM multi-level marketing

MLS multiple listing service

MS-DOS Microsoft disk operating system

MUD multi-user dimension

NAHB National Association of Homebuilders

NAR National Association of Realtors

NASD National Association of Securities Dealers

NASDAQ National Association of Securities Dealers Automated Quotation

NAV net asset value

NFA National Futures Association

NOI net operating income

NOW negotiable order of withdrawal

NPV net present value

NR not rated

NYSE New York Stock Exchange

OAR overall rate of return

OBL ocean bill of lading

OJT on-the-job training

OMB Office of Management and Budget

OPEC Organization of Petroleum Exporting Countries

OPM other people's money

OSHA Occupational Safety and Health Act

OTC over-the-counter

P&L Profit and Loss Statement

PC personal computer

PC-DOS personal computer disk operating system

P/E price/earnings ratio

PGIM potential gross income multiplier

PIC personal identification code

PIN personal identification number

POP point-of-purchase display

PPI producer price index

PPP point to point protocol

PREFAB prefabricated house

PSA public service announcement

PV present value

PUD planned unit development

R&D research and development

RAM random access memory

RAM reverse annuity mortgage

ROI return on investment

ROM read-only memory

RTC Resolution Trust Company

S&L Savings and Loan Association

SBA Small Business Administration

SBDC Small Business Development Centers

SBIR Small Business Innovation Research Program

SEC Securities and Exchange Commission

SEP Simplified Employee Pension

SVGA super video graphics array

SIPC Securities Investor Protection Corporation

SLIP serial line Internet protocol

SLMA Student Loan Marketing Association

SPEC on speculation

TCMP Tax Compliance Measurement Program

T&E travel and entertainment expense

TIN taxpayer identification number

TQM Total Quality Management

UPS United Parcel Service

USERID user identification

VA Veteran's Administration

VAT value added tax

VGA video graphic array

VP vice president

VRM variable rate mortgage

WPI wholesale price index

WWW World Wide Web

YTD year-to-date

NOTES

Notes

ABOUT THE AUTHOR

Liz Buffa joined The Princeton Review in 1989. She has taught classes in SAT, LSAT, GMAT and SAT-II special subject tests. She is a graduate of Wellesley College and lives in Locust Valley, NY with her husband and two sons, David and Paul. This is her fourth book for The Princeton Review.